Even More Days Of Heaven

Even More Days

of

Heaven

180 ways
to lift your spirits

SANDRA BRAY

A record of this publication is available from the British Library.

ISBN 978-1-910027-27-1

Typesetting by Wordzworth Ltd
www.wordzworth.com

Cover design by Titanium Design Ltd
www.titaniumdesign.co.uk

Cover image by the author.

Published by Local Legend
www.local-legend.co.uk

*This book is dedicated to my Mum, a great optimist,
who has always offered me encouragement throughout my life.*

Acknowledgements

My gratitude always to those whom I call my local spiritual heroes and from whom I continue to learn:

Julie Burke, Sally Parker, Alan Jones, Maureen Rolls, Ann Moore, Mary and Adrian Smith, Stephanie Parr, Tina Murt, Sue Wearne, Louise Russell, Jackie Blakewell, Deborah Grant and Angie Kruger. I am also greatly indebted to Nigel Peace of Local Legend for his expertise and guidance.

About the Author

Sandra Bray has worked for the Royal Air Force, the National Health Service and as a college lecturer. After a series of life-changing events she redirected her energies to holistic therapy, the Tarot and in facilitating workshops. The Celtic traditions and folklore, and the countryside and coastline of her home county of Cornwall, UK, continue to inspire her in a new and fulfilling life.

Sandra can often be seen swimming in the sea during the summer months with her German Shepherd dog.

Sandra's website is *https://www.sange888.com*

Previous Publications

Odd Days of Heaven (ISBN 978-1-910027-17-2): runner-up in the 2016 Local Legend national Spiritual Writing Competition.

This Book

Sandra Bray's highly original debut book, 'Odd Days of Heaven', offered inspiration and guidance for those on a spiritual path by suggesting ideas, projects and themes to pursue for every other day of the year – the odd-numbered days. 'Even More Days of Heaven' now completes a full year of wisdom. These books represent an astonishing feat of research and of deep spiritual awareness, a genuine and unique gift to us all.

This is a book that may be dipped into at any point, but quite a few of the suggestions are specific to their dates of entry so it may be a good idea to check a little way ahead. "Feel free," says Sandra, "to ignore any suggestions that do not resonate with you – but please don't be afraid to move out of your comfort zone occasionally!"

Grounding and Protection

When adopting any new spiritual practice such as the suggestions offered here, it is important to feel grounded and protected, staying in the present and maintaining a good energetic vibration. For some, protection may involve prayers to God (or Source, or the Creator, or the Higher Self), calling in spirit guides or invoking guardians of the four directions, to name a few practices. There are other suggestions within this book. We also need to know that our body is safe and in a safe environment, so cleansing the space where we meditate or conduct any charm work, for example, is important; this can be done by smudging, sound healing or spraying holy water into the corners of the home.

Remember that *everything* is energy. Love is a vibrational energy so if we live and work with love and kindness then the energies around us – and attracted to us – are of similarly high vibrations. Please keep your heart and mind open and full of love as you work with the suggestions here.

Thus may you rediscover, as I have, your own Days of Heaven!

Contents

January

Woollen hats, mittens and red noses characterise this month and so we often remain indoors a good deal, reflecting on our resolutions and the commitments to change that we made recently at the New Year celebrations. At this time, many of us want to start planning a 'rebirth' and a new direction in life.

The January moon is known as the Wolf Moon. Important celebrations during this month are Carmentalia and the Feast of Hecate. There is further information about each month's moon and celebrations at the end of this book.

2ⁿᵈ January – Feng Shui

This is a good time for us to consider a few easy changes to enhance the harmony of our homes and the flow of abundance in our lives. There will be a new option to be considered each month. The basic purpose of Feng Shui is to create balance in the home and garden by using the energies of colour, plants and the placement of furniture. Today, why not try adopting some of these recommendations?

Let's start by creating a wealth corner, also known as a money corner, to encourage the journey of abundance towards us. The wealth corner would usually be in the far left corner of a room as it is entered and the most common room would be the living room. However, if the television, for example, is in this corner then it is not a good location and it is better to choose another room where the wealth corner would be clutter-free and able to hold items associated with financial abundance.

In this wealth corner, items to be placed could be a 'horn of plenty' (also known as a cornucopia) perhaps filled with our lottery ticket numbers or Premium Bonds, and some good luck charms: a citrine, aventurine or jade crystal would be good and maybe a money plant. A piggy-bank full of money (preferably gold or silver in colour) would be appropriate too. We can strengthen this money corner with the ways of Wicca, for example by writing "Thank you" in green ink on the back of raffle tickets to bring luck. If we're waiting to hear about a debt problem or mortgage decision, we could place the details in the wealth corner with the words "Thank you for helping me with this" to encourage a suitable resolution.

Dragons are considered very auspicious in Feng Shui so try to find a red dragon, a model or a picture, as an added bonus in the corner. In Celtic history, too, dragons gathered and protected treasure. It is important to keep this wealth corner clean and to ensure that there are no items of furniture creating a block in front of it so that the energies may flow freely towards it.

Helpful tip: There are many Feng Shui books available. However, try to find one that provides clear pictures and diagrams to help with understanding its basic concepts.

4th January – Quan Yin

In East Asian Buddhism, Quan Yin is the goddess of compassion and considered to be a Bodhisattva of compassion and mercy. Quan Yin means 'She who listens to the world's sounds'. Some icons of Quan Yin show her holding an infant and thus she has a strong resonance with Mother Mary of the Christian faith, as well as other beliefs where mother and child are represented. She is also sometimes seen carrying 'pearls of illumination' and pouring healing water from a vase, known as the water of life. The lotus flower is another symbol associated with Quan Yin and the mantra 'Hail to the Jewel in the Lotus', perhaps better known as *om mane padme hum*, can help us to remember the qualities of harmony, compassion and unconditional love that we all possess.

With the New Year now upon us, let us make an intention to think of Quan Yin's qualities often and to allow these to flow throughout our hearts so that our thoughts and actions contain these energetic vibrations. Allowing greater compassion – for others and ourselves – to enter our lives enables us to 'walk our talk' and steer ourselves with inner peace through daily life.

Helpful tip: We could occasionally do a short mantra meditation, repeating *om mane padme hum* (pronounced as omm mannee padmee humm) whilst holding a rose quartz crystal.

6th January – Greek Inheritance

This is the day when the Greek Orthodox Church celebrates Christmas, so today we could acknowledge the rich heritage of healing and the light of knowledge that the ancient Greeks bequeathed us. Their fables, myths and legends enrich our lives to this day, with great meaning and wisdom to be found in them. We continue to learn and to be inspired by the teachings of the philosopher Plato and the physician Hippocrates, for example. It was the latter who said, "Let food be your medicine and thy medicine shall be thy food." We should also not forget Galen, the Greek philosopher, physician and surgeon from the 2nd century AD, nor Pythagoras the mathematician, who greatly assisted the advancement of Maths so essential to modern technology.

Today, let us find a moment to spend a little quiet time contemplating the gifts we have benefited from that the ancient Greeks provided, whether they be our children's DVD of the film Hercules or reading Aesop's Fables to them, our holidays on a Greek island, our philosophical studies or our classical education. We can express our thanks for their part in the rich heritage of teachings and entertainment from which peoples throughout the world continue to benefit.

8th January – Spinning

In olden days, this is around the time when women returned to their spinning after the Yuletide festivities. Centuries ago, the task of spinning was considered an important role and was undertaken by the females of the household, with the girls starting at a young age in learning how to spin from their mothers and grandmothers. With the arrival of mechanisation and the industrial revolution, this work generally moved into the factories.

Today, let us consider that the poor working conditions of those in the mills of the UK many years ago are now still found in other countries where people, including children, are employed in dangerous and unhealthy environments. We could be mindful of these practices today and send our heartfelt thoughts for the wellbeing of the workers by lighting a candle and offering a prayer for them.

Perhaps we could set an intention only to purchase our clothes from ethical sources in future, to assist those in need.

10ᵗʰ January – Jet, the Capricorn Crystal

At various points in this book, I shall mention a crystal to obtain that can help us to make progress along our paths. Ensuring that we remain protected and grounded is important, especially when conducting any meditation or charm work. For January, we can start with jet which is one of the crystals associated with the astrological sign of Capricorn. Jet's qualities enhance protection and grounding, and at the same time can assist us in achieving our potential for personal and spiritual growth.

It is commonly recognised that Whitby jet is the best in the world. However, it is no longer commercially mined and is now sourced, as in ancient times, by allowing the sea naturally to erode the cliffs and uncover this black treasure. Whitby jet is found along the north Yorkshire coastline and was formed in the Jurassic era from an ornamental tree still seen in our parks and gardens and commonly known as 'the monkey puzzle' tree.

Research jet today and obtain a small piece to keep nearby, placed in the pocket or held in the hands when meditating or conducting any practices when grounding and protecting are required.

Helpful tip: If you are only able to purchase jet as an item of jewellery, it is important to cleanse the energetic vibrations of the previous owner or maker, as jet can easily soak up others' vibrations. A thorough cleansing can be carried out by initially placing the article in a singing bowl, if possible; when the bowl sings, the crystal may well shake and quiver – a good sign that it is releasing the old energies. The jet can alternatively be placed in dried lavender for a few days.

A pendulum can be used for 'yes' and 'no' answers so perhaps try this out with the jet to learn whether it has been thoroughly cleansed before using it. (There is much more on this method in my book *Odd Days of Heaven.*) To charge the crystal ready for use, it can be placed on a windowsill to soak up the sun's rays or left overnight under a full moon; many crystal healers use both the sun and the full moon.

12th January – Black and White Pebbles

Although the Christmas and New Year period is a time of celebration when families gather together, this can also occasionally lead to difficulties because of the varying personalities and characters of the people involved – perhaps arguments arise that lead to disappointments. Or maybe we just feel weighed down by old concerns and unable to use the celebratory energies of this time to start afresh. A potential way to uplift ourselves is to visit a beach (or any waterway, if not living near the sea) and collect a handful of black pebbles and one white pebble.

When we have our pebbles we sit down and cup the black pebbles in our hands, keeping the white one nearby. Then we name the concerns we have and 'hand them over' into the black pebbles one by one. If we're alone, we can even vocalise these concerns, pouring our hearts into the black pebbles; this can help to release a blockage we may have held back from expressing. Indeed, the pebbles may represent people we know who have disappointed us or hurt our feelings; not wishing to express our concerns to them in person, the black pebbles become their surrogates. Once we have released our thoughts and feelings into the black pebbles, we throw them into the water so that they disappear from view.

Then we pick up the white pebble and express our gratitude to the energies of the water for accepting our troubles, before throwing the white pebble into the water as our 'thank you' gift. While doing this we may wish to call upon the sea goddesses of Stella Maris, Doris or Thetis for their help, or Oshun if we're by a lake or river as she is a goddess of sweet waters. Wearing a blue scarf, blue tie or blue necklace can help the throat chakra to release blockages as we voice our concerns to the pebbles.

Helpful tip: If we don't live anywhere near a waterway, an option is to find the pebbles where we can and then bury them in the earth instead, ensuring that the place chosen is away from our homes, and ask the Great Mother for her help. Reiki healers may also wish to draw a healing symbol on the white pebble as a further gratitude for help from the loving universal energies.

14ᵗʰ January – Ribbon Colour Visualisation

Many of us have difficulty visualising colours and images when meditating, so today let's try practising this using ribbons. Let's start with the simple method of looking at a blue ribbon and, on closing the eyes, continuing to see it in our hands (look at it again if necessary to reinforce the colour). Now try visualising the wide expanse of a blue sky, a lovely gentle blue, spreading out way ahead to a far horizon. See it joining the blue sea, a different and slightly darker hue, and as we look at the sea we notice many changes of blue to turquoise and a bright blue-green colour. Then think of the clean and sharp colour of a deep blue sapphire crystal set as a flower pattern in a ring. Envision it changing to the baby blue colour of a forget-me-not flower, allowing the flower then to change to a bluebell, and note the delicate but darker shade of blue which is almost indigo.

Next, hold a white ribbon and with eyes closed visualise big white fluffy clouds against the backdrop of a blue sky, seeing their different shapes and watching them skim across the sky. Now change the view to the sea once again and see white surf cresting the waves, frothing on their way to shore. Change this view to the white curtain of a waterfall, such as Niagara Falls, and see the expanse of this waterfall sending puffs of white spray into the air. The spray now turns to ice crystals and falls on the ground as snow, producing a deep covering as if in the Arctic Circle.

Finally hold a green ribbon and, on closing the eyes, see the ribbon as a bright green blade of grass before allowing the vision to spread out into a large meadow with the boldness and brightness of the green grass vista before us. Then take in a view of trees in full leaf with bright green leaves fluttering in the breeze. Change the trees to holly trees and note their dark green shiny leaves, then to fir trees, and now see one fir tree full of Christmas ornaments with a fairy on top in the middle of the room where we are sitting, before opening our eyes.

These are a few examples of visualising colours and we can spend as long as we wish on each vision to help imprint it upon our mind's eye. We can include whichever colours we wish, along with any visual-isations, and then expand the practice to imagining textures and tastes.

Perhaps later we can even try visualising ourselves within a crys-tal or inside a tree, to explore these different environments… These practices can help with manifesting whatever we wish to attract into our lives.

Helpful tip: If ribbons are not available then substitute these with items of clothing or cloth. Another useful way to improve visualisa-tion is to close our eyes and think of our front door; this is something we see frequently and is imprinted upon our memory and thus easy to recall. The same can be said of the colours of a car or our living room sofa.

16ᵗʰ January – Jupiter's Glyph

Many of us have heard the classical music by Gustav Holst entitled 'Jupiter – bringer of jollity', part of 'The Planets' suite of music with

Jupiter being the seventh movement. Within this movement there is a particular hymn that has become very popular in recent years, entitled 'I Vow to Thee My Country'. In astrology, Jupiter is linked with good fortune, optimism, hope, luck, success and abundance. Its planetary glyph (or representative symbol) is a mixture of the figures 2 and 4 written together.

To take advantage of Jupiter's largesse, let us be a little artistic today and paint or draw Jupiter's glyph (an example is at the start of the January chapter). Then we can put it on view in our place of business or display it in our home as a pleasing reminder of luck, abundance and of being jolly and optimistic. We may even wish to paint a few of them and give them as cards to our family and friends as a way of sending them luck.

Helpful tip: When we go to the beach, it's a nice idea to write our wishes in the sand, especially in the form of a simple picture. To bring abundance to our home, we could draw the outline of a house adding Jupiter's glyph in the middle of it.

18th January – Carnation, the January Flower

Carnations belong to the flower family of dianthus, which also includes the popularly named Sweet William. The ancient Greeks named these flowers after Zeus, dianthus meaning 'Flower of Zeus', and called carnations 'the divine flower'. Most of us associate roses with love; however, carnations have this association too as they symbolise love and purity.

Carnations are one of the easiest flowers to grow from cuttings. Today, let's buy a bunch of carnations and sift through them to find stems where a new growth of leaves is forming. Gently pull these away from the main stem and place them in a clear glass jar with fresh water on a windowsill, then watch the roots grow. When the roots are approximately 2" (5 cm) long, plant them in pots ready for planting out in the spring. A supply of carnations to give with love as a small bouquet to others will probably be available by the end of the summer.

Helpful tip: A small clear quartz crystal popped inside the glass vase when rooting should help the carnation cuttings to root well. Or, as they are a flower of love, then a rose quartz crystal may be appropriate.

20th January – St Agnes

This is St Agnes' Feast Eve. St Agnes was devoted to religious purity and refused to marry as she deemed herself married to God. As punishment for her refusal to marry she was placed in chains, taken to a brothel (where it is said an angel protected her) and eventually condemned to death. St Agnes subsequently became the patron saint of virgins, chastity and young girls. Angels are mentioned in several faiths and in most faiths there is mention of protective divine energies.

From today, let us try asking our guardian angel each morning to protect us during the day; then on retiring to bed each night, we can thank them for being with us and offering their protection and guidance. If we have children, we can extend this request for them as they wake each day and on tucking them into bed to sleep at night. A simple prayer could be, "Dear angels, please shine your love and light upon me and my loved ones, bringing us protection, courage, joy, grace, healing, compassion, wisdom and tolerance. Thank you and bless you, so mote it be."

22nd January – Midwinter Festival

In Iceland, the Midwinter Festival of Thorrablot is a pagan festival linked with Thor, the Norse god of thunder, and takes place during the thirteenth week of winter. At this festival, the Icelandic people celebrate with family and friends gathering to eat, recite stories and poetry, and to dance and sing their traditional songs. Why not join in with this festival in our own homes and have a good time with family and friends, telling stories, dancing and singing? Or perhaps a small impromptu event such as a talent show could be organised where the local community can join in displaying their artistic talents. By now there are signs of the evenings becoming lighter after the Winter Solstice last month, so isn't that something to celebrate?

Helpful tip: Being an island race, the Icelandic people take advantage of the sea around them and create many dishes of seafood as part of their staple diet. In deference to this Icelandic festival we could include similar dishes as part of our event.

24th January – Tipsy Laird

Today we will make an easy pudding in preparation for Burns' Night tomorrow, when many Scottish people and Scottish descendants celebrate their national poet Robert Burns (born on the 25th January, 1759). History tells us that he came from farming stock and worked on his father's farm, later becoming a Customs Officer. Robert Burns wrote poems from an early age and many of us have probably used his phrases without knowing that the words were made famous by him. Examples are "my love is like a red, red rose", referring to a mouse as a "timorous beastie" and "the best laid plans of mice and men". The latter phrase reminds us of the title of John Steinbeck's classic book 'Of Mice and Men'; apparently, Steinbeck was influenced by a Burns poem for this title. 'Auld Lang Syne', sung by so many people on New Year's Eve, was also penned by Robert Burns.

The pudding we prepare today is a special trifle known as 'Tipsy Laird'. We make a trifle in the usual way but instead of adding sherry we add Scotch whisky! Depending upon how tipsy we want to feel tomorrow, we add a wee dram or a large dram of Scotch. We could also research Robert Burns' poems and recognise how much of his terminology we still use in our everyday language, lamenting that he died at the young age of thirty-seven years.

26ᵗʰ January – Snow Melt

January and February often see snowfall in the northern hemisphere. From today, keep watch for some snow and, when coming across a perfectly clean and untouched patch, scoop some into a jar, replace the lid and allow it to melt. Label the jar with the date it was collected and store it safely in a cupboard. If the snow melt is collected on a specific day, such as a saint's day, then make a note of this as well on the label. The reason for collecting snow melt is to use it for anointing our candles for magical or healing work. Or, if wishing to make an offering to a plant, a tree or to the land in general, then it will also be perfect for this.

When snowflakes fall to Earth they are beautifully formed crystals and the energy of these frozen crystals remains within the snow melt. It therefore lends this wonderful energy to our candles or to the land, offering them additional honour.

Helpful tip: If there are several snowfalls during these months, take advantage of them each time by collecting snow melt in jars. These can be kept for several years so if we do not have another snowfall for a while we would still have a supply for our ceremonial rituals.

28ᵗʰ January – National Storytelling Week

Around this time of the year is National Storytelling Week, with events taking place throughout the country and stories being relayed for the benefit of children and adults alike. We may have loved our stories when we were young and avidly read adventures written by Enid Blyton, Roal Dahl and more recently J K Rowling. The imagination and ingenuity of our favourite storytelling authors, who were able to immerse us in another world, is awe-inspiring.

If we have our own children or grandchildren who love to hear a story at bedtime, we may have wished that we could tell them a story from our own imagination rather than reading from a book. So let's use National Storytelling Week as the impetus to be creative in our own storytelling. We can utilise all sorts of images to help us, such as the clouds in the sky with the outlines of a swan, a fish or a lily-pad; there may also be a rainbow. Just think of a short story we could create from these by pretending that the swan is a good witch, the fish and a frog sitting on the lily-pad are her friends, and the angel of the rainbow is going to help her return to human form.

Another option is the after-dinner game of six dice, which have a simple picture on each side and thus a total of thirty-six pictures. As the game is passed around the table, each person throws the dice and according to which six pictures land upright the person must create a short story based on them. This game could be used instead for a child preparing for sleep; he or she throws the dice and then we then create a special bed-time story based around the pictures. The child, being integral to the outline of the story to be created, may adore this way of storytelling and feel very much a part of its creation.

Helpful tip: We could even try making our own similar game with dice, or with a spinner on a board. Examples of simple pictures to use could be a shoe, a bus, an aeroplane, a car, a star, a flower, a crown, a pipe, a cake, a candle, a hat, a horse, a cat… or anything else that comes to mind. Another alternative is to use a pack of playing cards with a plain sticky label on one side bearing a simple picture; each card in the pack could have an image and the child can then pick five or six cards from which the story can be created.

30ᵗʰ January – The Star in Tarot

In the Tarot, The Star is linked with Aquarius, which is associated with optimism, hopes, dreams, wishes being fulfilled, gifts and highest ideals. It is sometimes known as the Star of Hope. Today, let us think carefully about a wish we would love to see fulfilled; then on the next full moon we will go outside and make our wish to Selene, the moon goddess. As the Star of Hope is linked with the highest ideals, let us also make a wish for countries that are struggling with strife or famine, for our oceans to keep them clean and pure, and not forgetting the deforested areas of the world and our ice caps.

Vocalising our wishes as if they are already occurring, and expressing our thanks to the Star of Hope and the moon goddess for them, could be considered as 'a cosmic order' and a way to add power to our wishes. Keeping The Star Tarot card in view, or perhaps by our bedside, may also assist us in focusing on our planned wish while waiting for the next full moon.

Helpful tip: If we do not own a Tarot deck, an image of The Star can be sourced via the Internet.

February

There is a noticeable lengthening of the days despite this often being a very cold month. We are between winter and spring and for many of us February can feel as though the winter has been far too long and a change of climate is needed. We may be ready for brighter and longer days to arrive and it is important to maintain our health in this last month of winter.

February's moon is known as the Snow Moon. Festivals held this month are Imbolc, the Feast of Aphrodite, Terminalia, Lupercalia and Maha Shivrati.

2nd February – Chinese New Year

The Chinese New Year varies in date each year, being linked with the second new moon after the winter solstice. Today, let's take a leaf from their tradition of giving what's known as 'lucky money' to children in red envelopes decorated with gold. For this, we place a £2 ($2) coin in a red envelope and give one each to the children in our family as a gift of love and for abundance in their lives. These can then be kept as a talisman or a lucky charm by the children until the next Chinese New Year.

In numerology, the number two likes to be partnered so using this amount for the lucky charm can help to encourage prosperity.

Helpful tip: If we are artistic, we could make and design our own red envelopes. However, they can usually be purchased around this time from any local Chinese grocery shop; the benefit of these is that they have Chinese symbols in gold already embossed, denoting luck and abundance.

4th February – World Cancer Day

The colour pink has been linked with cancer charities and on this day we could try wearing the colour pink in support of the event – perhaps a pink scarf or hairband, a ribbon or an item of pink jewellery.

Also on this day, let's try a healing meditation, sending a pink ribbon out to the world. Firstly, we light a pink candle for love and compassion and as we do so express the intention for the light of the candle flame to send love, light and healing to all those suffering with cancer, also to their families and carers. We sit for a while in peace and stillness and prepare ourselves for a meditation with grounding and protection. We can be in our usual safe place and request the assistance of any guides and angelic helpers.

When ready, we visualise our crown chakra opening as if a lotus flower is unfurling its petals and a pillar of divine healing light is entering our body through the crown. This divine healing energy wishes to be sent out to the world through our heart centre. Now let us see our heart centre opening like a large pink rose with petals unfurling from the centre, out of which appears a pink ribbon that keeps on unfurling away from our body, out of the nearest window and eventually being so long that it is able to wrap itself around the Earth like a giant, pink-ribboned gift. Intend for the pink ribbon to infuse love and healing to all those suffering, whether human or animal, and especially those suffering with cancer.

When ready to close the meditation, we visualise the end of the ribbon fluttering away from the centre of the rose and the rose petals once again forming a tight bud as we close the heart chakra. Then we close our crown chakra with the lotus flower petals also closing to a tight bud. Wait a few moments before opening the eyes and being back in the room.

Helpful tip: As we are working with the higher chakras, it is important to maintain a good sense of grounding during this meditation, so placing a haematite crystal at our feet will help. Also, holding a rose quartz crystal and saying a short prayer of thanks for the healing sent to all those who needed it would finish this meditation nicely.

6th February – Waitangi Day in New Zealand

On the 6th February, 1840, the Treaty of Waitangi was signed with New Zealand becoming a British colony and guaranteeing the Maori people rights to their lands. The Maoris were the first inhabitants of New Zealand after voyaging thousands of miles across the Pacific Ocean. Today let us think of indigenous peoples throughout the world, with their rich cultural heritage, who have been displaced (whether centuries ago or more recently).

In our current world, many thousands have become refugees, fleeing conflict or famine and losing much including their family members. Let us light a candle for these refugees and for those who still work to maintain their cultures after displacement, with the intention for their safety and for peaceful solutions to their plight. If we wish to help refugees further, there are several organisations to which we can make donations or local collectives in our own towns where we might volunteer our help in collecting necessary items such as clothing for them.

8th February – A Spell for Luck

We all wish for luck and success in our lives whether it is in our work, studies or general finances, and today we can create our own spell. Firstly, have to hand a pen, a piece of paper, gold (or yellow) cotton, a gold drawstring bag, a shell, a feather, a small clear quartz crystal and a small piece of crushed cinnamon stick. Write on the paper:

> "I'm so very lucky, lucky, lucky, lucky. I'm so very lucky, it's true.
>
> I'm so very lucky, lucky, lucky, lucky. I'm so very lucky, thank you."

Then roll the paper up into a small scroll and tie it with the gold cotton. Place the scroll, shell, feather, crushed cinnamon and clear quartz crystal into the bag and tie the drawstring. Saying a few words of thanks for luck and success as though it is already received would assist the energy of the spell. Once complete, the bag can be placed in our handbag, desk drawer or perhaps in our cash box if we run a business. As an added factor for luck, the verse could be written in gold on red paper (following Chinese Feng Shui) or in gold on green paper (following Wiccan prosperity beliefs).

Helpful tip: Some may recognise the spell verse as similar to a popular Kylie Minogue song several years ago, called 'I Should be so Lucky in Love'. It may help to raise our energy in working with this spell if we sing the spell verse to this particular tune each day. For an extra boost, sing the verse three times to use 'the power of three'!

10th February – National Heart Month

In the UK, February is national Heart Month. What better way to spend today than in saying a mantra for our hearts: a simple example is "Peace in my heart, peace in my body, peace in my life." We can repeat this simple mantra during the course of the day, saying it silently or even singing it as we drive to work or when carrying out our daily activities. When we are at peace, life can flow effortlessly. Peace allows us to listen to our inner spirit and when our bodies are in peaceful repose there is a knock-on physical wellbeing effect for our heart and other organs.

Let us try to find some quiet moments during the day for breathing slowly. Feel peace surrounding us and filling the body so that the whole body is breathing and working in harmony. Peace is the scent of a rose garden, light fluffy clouds in a summer sky, the gentle lapping of waves on a seashore, a river gurgling downstream or garden birdsong. Allow the heart to be at peace today and continue with this practice for the sake of the heart.

Helpful tip: A pleasant activity that reminds us of our heartfelt gratitude and to do things we love is to draw a large heart outline and within it make a note of what brings love and enjoyment into our lives. (Also see the entry for the 20th September.)

12ᵗʰ February – Rowan Month
(21ˢᵗ January to 17ᵗʰ February)

The rowan tree (also known as mountain ash) is believed to offer protection as well as healing and success. It was connected with witchcraft in olden days and planted to keep evil away, often being seen outside homes and in churchyards. Many consider the rowan tree to represent a strong life-force energy. Being ornamental and graceful trees, they offer a pleasing aspect to our gardens with their feather-like leaves so perhaps we could plant one in the garden as a reminder to us of feeling strong and empowered by our own life-force. Rowan trees blossom from May onwards and their red berries, which are rich in vitamin C, can be seen in the autumn.

Last month on the 20ᵗʰ January, we asked the angels to protect us and our children; today, let us find a rowan tree and make a cross of protection for our homes from one of its twigs. It is important to approach the tree with respect and offer it a gift, such as spring water or snow melt poured onto its roots, or a crystal to bury in the earth as an expression of gratitude, before cutting a small twig of approximately 6" (15 cm) which can then be cut in half.

The crosses that we make are small and with equal arms of approximately 2" to 3" (5 - 8 cm) in length. They are tied with red cotton at the centre and whilst tying them together we whisper to the rowan cross our request for it to provide protection for the home. Once done, we could pass the rowan cross through incense smoke to charge and bless it before placing it at the entrance to the home, perhaps hung on a wall or above the door or standing upright on a shelf. It is an ancient belief that rowan crosses are effective in protecting our homes from unwelcome spirits.

Helpful tip: There are several entries in this book that suggest finding a certain tree or wild flower. If unsure how to recognise these, a good resource is 'The Spirit of the Hedgerow' by Jo Dunbar, which also describes the folklore and legends of our countryside as well as the medicinal properties of plants.

14th February – Commitments

This is St Valentine's Day and from its small beginnings in 18th century England until now it has become a big commercial event. The day celebrates St Valentine as the patron saint of love, and also of young people and happy marriages. St Valentine was a holy priest in Rome who performed marriage ceremonies for those who were forbidden to marry, and thus charged with not conforming to the rules of the Church and subsequently executed on 14th February, 270 AD. Here was a man who was committed to his convictions, despite the life-threatening outcome to his activities.

Let's think about our own commitments in life and spend a little time questioning ourselves as to whether some of our commitments are draining our energies. Have we spread ourselves too thinly and subsequently not given enough time to the few really important commitments? Are we feeling fettered to a certain project and believe our integrity will be questioned if we release ourselves from it now? The Temperance major arcana card in the Tarot can be associated with giving too much of ourselves with little or no time for our own pleasures, so that we spread our energies too thinly for anyone to benefit. We can use the Temperance card as a reminder for us to value ourselves and lead a more balanced life.

So today, we could reflect on how our commitments feel and decide which ones are important and which can be let go of or put on the back burner until we are able to give them proper time. This is not abdicating our responsibilities in life but making happy and healthy changes. Perhaps, instead, we could negotiate to lessen our commitment to certain activities so that we can maintain some involvement.

Consider whether we have been over-promising and under-delivering, thereby adding further stress.

Life is to be enjoyed. However, if there are too many commitments pulling at us and taking over our lives then we can potentially arrive at a state of dis-ease. St Valentine can remind us to be kind to ourselves – and to others, as they will also benefit from our efforts to maintain only those activities appropriate for us.

16th February – Totem Pouches and Medicine Bags

The ancients had their own totem pouches made from leather and mostly hung around their necks on a leather thong. They lived with the natural cycles of Mother Earth and honoured the land and all living upon it. They were spiritual in their recognition of nature and looked to their shamans for further spiritual insights and guidance for the wellbeing of their tribe or clan. Their totem pouches were their own form of physical acknowledgement of the guidance they believed they received from the spirits. For example, a tribesman may have been out hunting and an inspiration came to him to develop a new form of hunting tool. Perhaps he noticed a small piece of pyrite glinting in the sunshine at his feet and viewed this as a sign from the spirits that he could develop a new tool using this. So he would assign the pyrite a status and honour it by putting a piece into his totem pouch.

Let us try making our own totem pouch today (although not necessarily from leather) to hang on our bedpost or to keep in our pocket or handbag. Each time we feel that on our life's journey some item found at a specific place has a relevance to our progress, then we can place it in our totem pouch. For example, we may be at a beach meditating and receive a sudden insight about a matter that has plagued us for several months; then we could choose a small shell or pebble from the beach and place in the pouch.

Helpful tip: Some prefer to use a 'medicine bag' which they can create and decorate themselves. These bags are a little larger than totem pouches but fulfil a similar purpose. The Native American culture provides many examples of medicine bags that holds items of significance, some of which could be seeds, feathers or animal teeth, and other items relating to their personal vision quest.

18th February – A Psychic Development Group

To expand our psychic awareness and intuition, joining an established psychic development group is recommended as it could help us develop our spiritual learning in a safe and supportive setting. We could join an Open Circle at our local Spiritualist Church or check out other groups in the local area offering what we seek. Many find the support offered within a group, from its leaders and others attending, to be very beneficial. The group setting can also offer us the grounding and protection necessary for new learning.

There is so much to be learned about the mysteries of life and, whilst books and the Internet are useful resources, the opportunities of exploring with others enrich our experience. Personal experiences can be shared and we may be surprised to find that we also have something to offer that can enhance others' journeys. Group members often form close bonds of friendship in which trust plays a key part. Groups will frequently send absent healing during their sessions for those in need, whether individuals or specific areas of the world suffering distress.

Helpful tip: A good group should be welcoming and supportive and offer a safe learning experience where we can feel at ease and be comfortable. If this is not felt then we should leave this particular group and seek another that does fulfil these basic requirements.

20th February – Feng Shui

This simple tip is one that has been reinforced many times in many books: it is that of always closing the lid of the toilet as it is believed that our luck drains away down the pan whenever the toilet is flushed and the lid is left up. Taking this a step further, we should always ensure that the toilet or bathroom door is closed.

Even though our bathrooms and shower rooms are places where we cleanse ourselves, it is considered that our luck and abundance can drain away down the plug holes so it is wise to keep these doors closed. This is relevant for the main bathroom and any other ablution areas such as an en-suite shower room or small toilet facility in the hallway. For those whose bathroom or toilet door is immediately opposite the front door, this is especially recommended due to ease with which the energy of luck can flow out.

22nd February – Listening

George Washington, the first president of the USA, was born on 22nd February, 1732. History tells that one of his best characteristics was being able to listen to others before making decisions. However, what about listening to his own inner conscience in respect of his black slave maidservant, Oney Judge? The story goes that Oney escaped from the Washingtons' home when she learned that she was to be given away as a wedding gift, to live in the southern states. A federal customs officer was tasked to return her to the Washingtons' Philadelphia home; however, the story says that this officer listened to Oney's pleas to remain free. In actively listening to her, he probably also listened to his own inner conscience and subsequently did not carry out his instructions, thereby leaving Oney free for the rest of her lifetime.

From today, let us pay attention to our own listening skills. Do we allow others to finish speaking or do we interrupt them? Do we actively listen with our full attention or are we distracted by other events or people? It is respectful to listen properly to others and we will probably find that respect is then reciprocated. Also, like the federal customs officer, let's pay attention to our inner conscience and perhaps not listen so much to our ego! There are so many things we can learn in life simply by listening to others and to our heart.

Helpful tip: Active listening is a skill that can be learned by us all and many healthcare professionals are taught these skills to improve communication between patient and clinician. This includes observing body language. Perhaps this is also something that could be researched further, especially if we have a specific issue where active listening techniques could help.

24th February – Blessing (revisited)

In my earlier book 'Odd Days of Heaven', I referred to Pierre Pradervand's book entitled 'The Gentle Art of Blessing' and today let's revisit this but in a more creative way. We could create our own poetry by writing blessing verses for others such as wishes for healing, weddings, anniversaries or the birth of a child. We may also wish to try writing a verse that reflects our own thoughts of feeling blessed, such as our gratitude for the companionship of our pets, for our family or our relationship with angelic energies. Our blessing verses could be written on a blank card for that special someone, offering them a personal greeting.

A blessing verse for healing could be completed as a scroll and placed on our healing altar, or perhaps a house blessing verse could be given as a gift for family or friends who have moved to a new home. The choices are many so feel free to create whatever suits your desires. Ruth Burgess' book 'A Book of Blessings: and how to write your own' is an informative resource as a starting point. Blessings can be long or short, serious or light-hearted, and it's not necessary to make the verses rhyme. A simple example is this 'Blessing for Inner Light':

> "Bless my light indwelling so it may shine forth as a beautiful beacon.
>
> Bless it shining in my heart, reaching out to all I meet.
>
> Bless its radiance divinely sourced, creating harmony along its journey and bless the Great Spirit for sharing this gift."

Another resource is Claire Nahmad's book 'Make your own Angel Blessing Scrolls' in which we are guided with various Celtic deities and angels to be added to our blessing scrolls, such as Brigid (a fire goddess) and Columba for a house blessing.

Helpful tip: Pierre Pradervand's book '365 Blessings to Heal Myself and the World' may be of further help.

26th February – Make a Dreamcatcher

The Native Americans have a profound respect for the natural world and one of its myths is that of the spider goddess, Grandmother Spider, who spun the world into creation, spinning all the living people, animals and plants into existence. Dreamcatchers are seen regularly at MBS fayres and spiritual shops in the High Street, ranging from the very small to the more complex and large ones in various colours. The dreamcatcher, when hung above the bed, is said to protect us from nightmares as we sleep, only allowing good dreams through its web and thus aiding restful slumber.

Let us try making our own dreamcatcher today. We could start from scratch, but it may be easier to purchase a simple one from a shop and add our own embellishments; specific colours may also be chosen that match our décor. Dreamcatchers usually have the four elements represented of earth, air, fire and water hanging from the lower half as charms. For example, feathers represent air, shells represent water, a crystal for earth and a metal object to represent fire (as it would have been moulded to its shape using the heat of fire). Within the web of the dreamcatcher, Grandmother Spider is represented by sewing in place a black crystal with a spider painted on it.

To make the dreamcatcher personal to our desires, we can add feathers that are meaningful to us such as those from a swan to represent high spiritual qualities or perhaps from an owl to represent spiritual wisdom. Choose crystals associated with our aspirations, such as turquoise (linked to the sky gods and used greatly by the Native Americans), and if possible seek out shells from a favourite beach rather than buying them from a shop. Add whatever metal object is relevant, perhaps a mini Buddha figure to represent a desire for spiritual enlightenment would be a good choice.

Once complete and happy with what has been created, we then smudge it within the smoke of an incense stick or a white sage smudge stick to cleanse it and then bless it with our intentions. If there is a child in the family who suffers with nightmares, perhaps carry out this activity with them so that they can create their own dreamcatcher and be reassured on going to bed at night.

Helpful tip: The dreamcatcher is to hang freely above the bed and not against the wall.

28th February – Surprises

We all enjoy pleasant surprises, large or small, and they can help to lift our spirits. Pleasant surprises can be in the form of an unexpected bunch of flowers as a 'thank you' gift or perhaps finding a coin on the pavement or winning a prize in a raffle we had forgotten about because the ticket was purchased several months previously.

From today, let us try practising the request of pleasant surprises such as when having a family day out, going to a car boot sale or planning a special shopping trip with friends. An example of a request could be:

> "Dear angels (or universe), I am going out today with my friends and it would be lovely for me to have a wonderful surprise (or a great bargain). Thank you so much – so mote it be."

This request is similar to 'a cosmic order' but is a non-specific request and therefore open to serendipity arriving in an unexpected way, bringing a bubbling joy rising up within us. When the pleasant surprise arrives, it is important to thank the angels (or universe) for their benevolence. When we have tried this a few times and realised that it does work, we should try spreading the idea to our family and friends so that when we go out as a group for the day everyone can try making their own request – then wait and see what magic happens!

March

This is a month when the Spring Equinox brings a balance of equal daylight and night-time hours. Our spirits are uplifted and there is much looking forward.

March's moon is the Hawk Moon and festivals celebrated this month are Eostre (or Ostara), Liberalia, the Feasts of Athena and of Rhiannon, Shunbun no Hi and also Mothers' Day in the UK.

2nd March – Sacred Geometry

Sacred geometry surrounds us from the common flowers of our gardens to the beautiful nautilus shells of the ocean and the planets traversing the solar system, leaving patterns in their wake as they orbit. Sacred geometry has been called 'the root language of creation'. The geometric shapes created are truly awe-inspiring and yet we often travel through life unaware of them and their impact on our lives and our activities.

Looking more closely, we may wonder at the way flowers form into beautiful and perfect shapes, and the well-formed patterns of common little spiral shells found on our local beaches. Time-lapse photographs of the nightly movement of stars reveal many amazing patterns; indeed, the orbit of Venus around the Earth forms an exquisite pentagon.

Sacred geometry is based on the numbers in the Fibonacci Sequence, a mathematical model of growth: 1, 1, 2, 3, 5, 8, 13, 21, 34, 55, 89… Each number depends on the two before it. So for example, many flowers have 5 or 8 petals whilst the head of a sunflower has two interlocking spirals of seeds, 55 one way and 89 the other. The 'logarithmic spiral' of the nautilus shell (and snail!) is created mathematically by these numbers, and ratios of them are found in the (5-sided) pentagon and starfish. In history, this led to the association of the pentacle with magical practices. Because these ratios are 'natural' and pleasing to the eye, architects ancient and modern have used them in their designs, from the Parthenon in Greece to Notre Dame Cathedral and the United Nations Secretariat building.

Today, let us research sacred geometry (search the Internet for 'Golden Ratio') to gain further insights into the beautiful building blocks of our universe as one more way of expressing our gratitude for incarnating on this incredibly beautiful planet.

Helpful tip: Some years ago, the Spirograph was a favourite pastime for many a child, spending hours creating geometric mandalas, and it is still available. 'The Flower of Life' sacred geometry pattern is also popular for crystal grids and 'Archangel Metatron's Cube' is well known by those who study angels.

4th March – Psychic Signature

Our handwriting, including our signature, represents energy and, depending on how we write, this energy can block or allow the universal flow. Graphologists are skilled in understanding character, personality and other attributes from our handwriting. From whether our letters are upright or slanting to left or right, whether we write large or small, use loops or draw a circle for the dot over the letter 'i', much can be gleaned. Some organisations even employ graphologists for their advice when considering offering employment to a person who would be taking up a responsible position, in a similar way to psychological profiling. Also, forensic analysis of handwriting is often done by graphologists in criminal proceedings and court cases.

Today, perhaps we could adopt one change in our handwriting in order to allow the flow of universal energy to enter our lives. This concerns the letter 'g'. It involves leaving a slight gap in the top circle half and having a generous loop in the bottom half of the 'g' that comes right up again close to the top circle ready to start the next letter. An example of this can be seen in the picture for March. Writing the letter in this way encourages abundance into our lives, as the slight gap in the top circle allows abundance to fall into this circle and the generous loop in the bottom half indicates fullness.

Helpful tip: With a serious study of graphology, it is possible over time to identify strokes in our writing that represent undesirable characteristics, such as impatience or carelessness, for example. Then we can begin to improve ourselves, starting by deliberately changing our handwriting.

6th March – Simple Ribbon Knot Charms

Ribbon knot charms are easy to do and consist of setting a good outcome for our intentions, done with loving kindness. (Intending harm to others simply doesn't work!). As each line of the charm is spoken, a simple knot is tied in a length of ribbon. The number of knots used can vary; some prefer nine knots as it is 'the power of three by three' and is felt to be more potent. The power of three is relevant to many belief systems, including the Holy Trinity of Christianity, the Triple Goddess of Wicca and the Three Lucks or Cosmic Trinity of Chinese metaphysics. The colour of the ribbon is relevant too: use white for purity, black for binding, red for passion and energy, yellow for study and mental power, blue for healing and harmony, green for fertility and growth, purple for spirituality, pink for love and affection, gold for happiness and success and orange for creativity and justice.

There are many recorded verses and it is quite possible to create our own. However, a traditional verse is this:

"By knot of one this charm is begun.

By knot of two the charm will come true.

By knot of three so may it be.

By knot of four magical power I store.

By knot of five this charm is alive.

By knot of six this charm I fix.

By knot of seven blessing is given.

By knot of eight bound by fate.

By knot of nine this charm is mine."

However, some prefer to tie a number of knots relevant to what they are wishing to bring about. Generally, these are: one for focus, two for balance, three for timing, four for health, five for willpower, six for success, seven for love, eight for communication, nine for emotions and ten for endurance.

While waiting for the outcome, keep the knotted charm in a safe place and do not undo any of the knots. Usually a moon cycle of twenty-eight days will bring about a change. After the desired outcome, a ceremonial burning of the knotted ribbon or burying it in the earth, with thanks to the universe for its help, is a good thing to do.

Helpful tip: Any charms we create are helped along when we undertake positive activities to bring about changes for the end result. This enables us to maintain the energy of the charm and helps us to focus on achieving the outcome. A word of advice, though: after carrying out a charm, it is best not to discuss our actions with others as this dissipates the charm energy that has developed, so any empowerment we have provided to the charm becomes diminished and it is likely to fail. Once the outcome has been achieved, then feel free to let family and friends know!

8ᵗʰ March – International Women's Day

From humble beginnings with the Suffragettes in the UK in 1911, International Women's Day has blossomed throughout the world, encouraging many aspects of equality such as for pay, opportunity, education, training and employment. We are seeing more females in high-profile roles in business, politics and other professions and some companies even fund events held to promote female entrepreneurs. We can see female support groups in many cities or counties, with businesswomen coming together to help one another and encourage further growth in this area.

Many women seek support from our female counterparts in, for example, mother and toddler groups, a weekly gathering of friends at a café for a morning coffee or by becoming 'ladies who lunch'. However, what is becoming very popular are gatherings of like-minded females who form open groups commonly known as 'sister circles'. In these safe settings, women are able to release their emotional burdens to the circle, with each member taking a turn. One activity is to write down three things one wishes to remove from their life; once everyone has done this, the lists are ceremoniously thrown into a fire. Afterwards, intentions are set for change. Sometimes there is free dancing or the playing of various instruments, and afterwards the group may be led in a meditation, followed by tea and biscuits. The final part of the meeting might involve going outside to greet the rising moon.

The camaraderie of these circles, where women gather from all walks of life, is clearly evident with much laughter between strangers who are happy to express their fears and desires with trust that what occurs inside the circle remains within it. These circles are therefore a wonderful way to make new friendships and to find time for a little peace and support. They also help us to understand that in life we all have difficulties, upsets and challenges, and we are not alone in encountering these as we are human and it is part of our natural journey. Being in such company enables us to feel part of a supportive community.

Today, why not look into one of these groups in the local area. They may advertise on Facebook, at the local library, town or village hall, in a health food shop, at the venue itself or by word of mouth. For those who cannot get out and about, there are similar 'sister circles' online. Let us give one of these a try and see if it helps us to meet up every so often for some female-time.

Helpful tip: Let's not forget the men in our world! There are similar groups for men, too, where a spirit of comradeship can be gained and the more mature men can naturally take on the status of an 'elder', passing on their experience so that the younger ones learn about life in general in a safe and supportive setting.

10th March – Feng Shui

Grand houses, stately homes and palaces often have wonderful crystal chandeliers and whilst these are beautiful to look at they would be unrealistic for the vast majority of our homes. In the years after World War II, two-tier miniature chandeliers made from clear resin became popular as people recovered from the tough times and rationing and wished to beautify their homes.

Whilst these miniature chandeliers were not of genuine crystal, it is still possible for us to recreate our own authentic miniature crystal chandelier to suspend from the ceiling near the entrance of our homes. It is considered good Feng Shui for a crystal chandelier to be situated at this point to encourage opportunity, growth and abundance to enter the home.

Today, look into purchasing three individual crystals, with hanging hooks, from a local crystal shop and suspend them near the entrance. As we watch their faceted rainbow reflections create beauty and movement, we know that at the same time they are fulfilling another worthwhile energetic draw for us.

Helpful tip: It is important to dust these crystals weekly to maintain their sparkly energies of attracting abundance.

12th March – World Kidney Day

There is a well-known Taoist meditation that focuses on visualising the organs of our bodies smiling. Today, let us try a little of this ourselves and visualise our kidneys changing shape to form a smile as they sit either side of our spine, as though smiling at each other and basking in glowing health. If it seems difficult to see the kidneys smiling, then first focus on what our face looks like when we smile; see our eyes light up and our face soften and notice the gentle curve of the lips. Then try to imprint this image on the kidneys.

We can finish the meditation with a short prayer of thanks for our own health and ask for blessings to be poured upon all those specifically suffering from poor kidney health, that they may continue to receive the medical support and care they require.

14th March – Angelic Cleansing of our Homes

When we leave our homes for the day, for example to go to work, we generally check to ensure that unnecessary electrical items are switched off, the windows are closed and the doors locked. However, this period of absence can be a time when we ask the angels for their help in cleansing our home spiritually. A simple way to do this on leaving for the day is to say, "Dear angels, please shine your love and light in every area and every room of my home. Thank you."

Asking the angels to shine divine love and light into our homes sets the intention for their wonderful energies to permeate each room, providing cleansing and blessings ready for our return home later in the day. This is something we could adopt from today; perhaps also have a chat with friends to see whether they do something similar, as they may use different phrasing which feels more comfortable for us to use. After starting this practice, we may find that our homes feel a little more uplifting on our return and we sense 'something' intangible, a slight difference in the atmosphere, the home feeling a little lighter.

Helpful tip: Expressing our gratitude for the angels' help is important so we mustn't forget to say a little 'thank you' to them on arriving home for lightening the energy of our homes.

16th March – National Salt Awareness Week

This date usually falls within National Salt Awareness Week, when the use of excessive salt in our foods is publicised by health officers in order to guide us in using less, to help maintain healthier bodies. Salt has been used for thousands of years to preserve and flavour our foods and, whilst we require a certain amount of salt, it has become clear to health experts that we are consuming too much. Using herbs to flavour our food instead, cutting down on processed foods and preparing our own with fresh ingredients can all help to reduce our salt intake.

When buying salt, we should seek out the purest form by paying attention to the production processes it has undergone. Natural sea salt and low-sodium varieties are good choices.

There are many superstitions associated with salt through the ages, probably due to it being a food preservative and therefore very precious. For example, spilling salt was deemed unlucky and to mitigate any bad luck some of the spilt salt was thrown over the left shoulder (supposedly into the eye of the devil); many continue with this action today. It was also believed that salt could guard our babies and livestock against witches. Salt continues to be used as a means of cleansing in magical and religious practices.

However, let us also look at the beneficial health properties of salt. A simple example of this is the popular Himalayan salt lamp, which when lit helps to purify the air in our homes. We could also research halotherapy, which is an ancient natural treatment for respiratory illnesses and skin conditions by being in a 'salt cave microclimate'.

Helpful tip: Pink Himalayan salt, obtainable from health food stores, is considered one of the purest salts available and this could be a preferred option when adding salt to our food.

18th March – Shunbun no Hi

Around this time of the spring equinox falls Shunbun no Hi, a national holiday in Japan when the ancestors are honoured and families visit their graves to lay flowers as a mark of respect. In the West nowadays, many families are not able to visit the graves of their loved ones due to distance or for other reasons; so a way that we can join in with Shunbun no Hi is to make an offering, similar to a cloutie, to hang in the garden or on a nearby tree where it will not affect the wildlife.

We do this by making what is known in Mexico as *Ojos de Dios* (in Spanish this means the Eye of God), originally made by the Huichol Indians. As we make these we can recall the happy times we spent with our passed over family members, feeling warmth and gratitude as we remember their care and nurture of us as we grew from children to maturity, honouring their guidance. We may remember specific outings and parties, perhaps a big family wedding when we were all together and enjoyed being with many distantly-related family members.

An *Ojos de Dios* is made with two wooden sticks of equal length, approximately 6" (15 cm). We place one stick over the other to form a cross and secure this shape by knotting it in place with some wool. We then carry on using the wool to weave in and out of the four arms, similar to simple basketry, and in doing so we create a diamond formation. The weaving stops around ½" (1.25 cm) from the end of each arm. We can be creative as we wish, with different coloured wools incorporated into our weaved pattern, and perhaps a tail can also be added by plaiting the different coloured wools together.

Once completed we can hang them as suggested, or perhaps some may prefer to place them on 'ancestor altars' as our mark of respect and honour.

Helpful tip: The wooden stirring sticks commonly offered in cafés to stir our beverages are the perfect size for making our *Ojos de Dios*.

If unsure how to make them, there are pictures and instructions on the Internet.

20th March – Egg Decorating at Ostara

This is a fun activity to do with family and friends today and of course it has a pagan spiritual meaning as well, since eggs symbolise renewal, life-force energy and the fertility that is becoming evident at spring-time. Ostara (or Eostre) is the Germanic goddess celebrating fertility, renewal and rebirth, and is of course the origin of the name Easter.

Decorating eggs with colour, ribbons, glitter, feathers and symbols is an activity that brings people together; afterwards they can be hung on an 'egg tree' and become a focal point on our altar, if we have one, or perhaps on a windowsill. Egg trees can be attractive and pleasing to the eye when completed and can remain in place for the rest of the month. An egg tree is made by collecting some long twigs, which have fallen naturally in preference to cutting them straight from a tree. Bind the twigs together so that they spread out like a tree and place them in a jar or vase; then tie the eggs to the branches with cotton.

If we wish to give a painted egg to a friend for Easter, perhaps decorate one of them with images of the Feogh rune, which represents wealth.

Helpful tip: It is believed that burying a raw egg near the entrance to the home at this time encourages growth and fertility in the garden. Some say that it encourages abundance for the forthcoming year, in which case perhaps adding the Feogh rune sign to this egg before burying it will enhance this energetic vibration.

22nd March – World Water Day

Around this time is World Water Day. Dr Maseru Emoto (who passed to spirit in 2014) was a man of international reputation for his work with water, revealing the beautiful crystal shapes in frozen water when exposed to positive thoughts and emotions such as love. He also demonstrated misshapen crystals when the frozen water was exposed to ugly or hateful energy. It has long been thought that water retains memory and if we consider homeopathic remedies, in which the more a remedy is diluted the stronger it becomes, we can understand the possibility of this energy retaining memory.

When we show or express love to water, there is an element of healing that takes place within the water, so from today a new practice can perhaps be adopted. We may wish to use this for our pets, especially when travelling in the car, by carrying a refill water bottle with us so they have access to 'healed' water.

The way to achieve this is by drawing Reiki or other healing symbols – such as the simple word 'love' or a heart image – on the sticky side of labels and then fixing the labels to a bottle so that the symbols are on the inside, continuously sending healing to the water. Then we hold the bottle and send loving thoughts to the water. This is a simple practice to adopt also for the water we consume at home.

Helpful tip: Consider using a blue glass bottle for the storage of healed water as blue has long been recognised as a healing colour.

24th March – The Emperor in Tarot

In the Tarot, The Emperor major arcana card is linked with the astrological sign of Aries and represents a soul who has incarnated many times and as such has accrued much wisdom. However, it is in accessing that knowledge and wisdom where our task lies, for it is mostly in the subconscious mind.

Today, let's try to focus upon our intuition in general and the ways we can achieve this such as via our dreams, sensing our body's responses and feeling with our gut instincts. Another way is to find time for meditating and 'going into the quiet'. Meditation has a subtle effect of allowing our intuitive thoughts to come to the fore; when at peace, insightful moments arise and a solution to something often arrives. An easy way for some of us is to daydream when we are quite happy to sit and stare out of a window with softened eyesight and allow all sorts of thoughts to dance gently through our minds, and when in this state a thoughtful insight arises.

Helpful tip: 'Living Magically: a new vision of reality' by Gill Edwards and 'Instant Intuition' by Anne Jirsh may be helpful books to consider reading. The crystals labradorite, which assists with contemplation and introspection, and selenite, which can aid us in understanding any previous subconscious thoughts being brought to the surface, can be useful too.

26th March – Extra Spring Cleaning

When we have completed the usual spring clean in our homes, how about now trying a 'spiritual spring clean' of them? Following a Wiccan tradition, with our household broom (although a besom would be preferable) we brush from right to left throughout our homes and conduct this heading in the direction of the front door. This is not simply for the purpose of brushing the floors clean of physical dust but to brush away any 'energetic debris' which has become stale whilst remaining in our homes over the colder months.

Afterwards we can open the windows in every room then ring a bell three times in each corner (a Tibetan singing bowl could also be used). When doing so, go around the room in a clockwise direction. The sound from the bell helps to shift stuck energies in the corners, which leave via the open windows and doors. As a final spiritual spring clean, spray each room, including each corner (again in a clockwise direction) with a home-made spritzer of frankincense essential oil and water. While spraying, we can request the universe or a special deity to bless our home and all who live in it.

Helpful tip: If we don't own a bell or a singing bowl, we can clap our hands instead or maybe use a cut crystal glass and make it sing by adding a little water into the glass, dipping a finger into the water and then tracing around the lip of the glass with a finger.

28th March – St Teresa of Avila

This Roman Catholic saint, also called St Teresa of Jesus, was a Carmelite nun born on 28th March, 1515. She wrote 'The Way of Perfection' which, similar to the words of Hildegard of Bingen, described her experiences in prayer and how spiritual perfection can be attained by prayer. St Teresa said, "The important thing is not to think much but to love much and so to do whatever best wakens you to love."

From today, let us focus more on loving much! Love ourselves, our family, our friends, work colleagues, our wider community. Love our pets and all living creatures, love the environment they rely upon for their existence. Love our food and the food around the world so that it is infused with love as well as nourishment. Love our work, our hobbies and interests. Love the life-giving sun as it rises each day. Love the morning, the afternoon and the evening. Love the land, the mountains, the deserts, the rivers, seas and oceans. When life becomes a little busy and stressful for us we can stop and follow St Teresa of Avila's advice and "love much" instead and do that which "wakens you to love".

30th March – Alder Month (18th March – 14th April)

The alder tree is associated with the balance of masculine and feminine energies, grows in wet soil as well as dry, and can be seen growing along riverbanks helping to protect the surrounding land against erosion. During the alder month, Mother Earth is reawakening for another cycle of growth and regeneration and this is a time for bringing our plans closer to fruition. It also falls within the spring equinox period when the days and nights are of equal length and so a sense of balance is held in nature. Let us today follow Mother Earth's lead and bring balance to our lives in preparation for our plans coming to fruition.

When we are out of balance, it can be difficult dealing with everyday stresses and we can find that life in general becomes a battle; what we previously dealt with quite easily can become so much harder to find a solution for. When in balance we are better able to cope with the curve balls that life throws us and we are able to maintain a sense of wellbeing, leading to balance that assists us in igniting our plans.

To help create this balance in our lives at a practical level, perhaps we could consider taking up tai chi for the balance of spirituality and physical wellbeing. Or perhaps we can look at any areas in our home décor that are out of balance, with too much of one colour, and instead create a yin-yang balance with simple remedies such as a few cushions or a new rug in a different colour.

April

A tree relevant this month in our parks and gardens is the beautiful cherry blossom, which people often call 'Mother Nature's own confetti'. Many of us wish for calm breezes in order to experience the beauty of the cherry blossom for as long as possible before the April showers and gusting winds strip the trees of their blossom.

April's moon is called the Seed Moon. Some festivals this month are the Floralia, Veneralia, the Feast of Cybele, the Festival of Ceres, Norse Nine Nights and the Feast of Walburg.

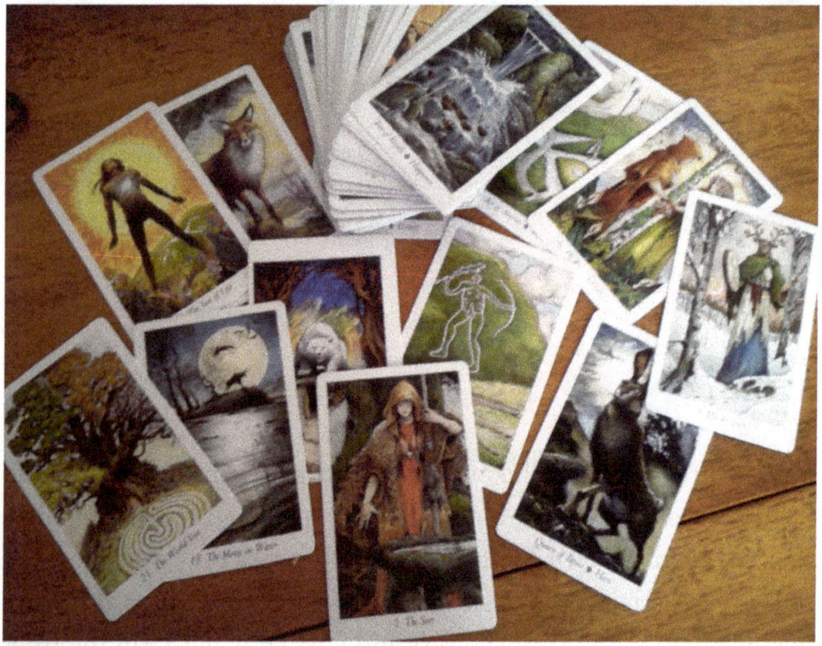

APRIL

2ⁿᵈ April – Daisy, the April Birth Flower

A bright and cheery flower with many daisy chain necklaces being created, the daisy is seen by some to be the flower of innocence and survival. How often do we see a daisy lawn being mowed and then a few days later up pop the daisies once again? The daisy's ability to grow and flower in adverse conditions is an inspiration to us all. Today, let us be prepared to think about daisy's qualities that we can adopt for ourselves in preparation for when life throws up a challenge for us, to be overcome by maintaining our tenacity and brightness and keep cheerful thoughts in our minds, knowing that the time will pass and we can flourish again just like the daisy.

A popular old song 'Accentuate the Positive' by Johnny Mercer in the 1940s may help us as the lyrics include "eliminate the negative… latch onto the affirmative… spread joy up to the maximum…" Doesn't this describe the daisy well? Research the song and its tune and it could turn out to be a go-to song when a lift is needed.

4ᵗʰ April – Dr Martin Luther King Jr

This great man who encouraged peaceful action when faced with injustice was born on 15ᵗʰ January, 1929, and assassinated on 4ᵗʰ April, 1968. In his "I have a dream…" speech of 28ᵗʰ August, 1963, he stated "All men are created equal." However, let us expand this simple but powerful phrase so that equality applies to many areas in our lives, not only in legislation concerning race, age and disability.

In our interactions throughout this year, let us consider equality from the perspective that life and universal energy connects us all and therefore all of life on this planet is equally deserving of respect and is sacred, as observed by many indigenous peoples throughout the world. Science has stated that we have the same chemicals in our bodies as the planets and so the old saying that we are 'made of stardust' has come home to roost. Making a good habit of remembering this interconnectedness each day may enable us to bring to the fore a respect for equality of all life on this wonderful planet throughout our daily lives and we can allow this to shine like a beacon to others.

6th April – Blowing a Healing Kiss

When we hear that friends and family are feeling under the weather, many of us send a prayerful request for them. We are often separated by distance and do not have the opportunity to visit them, taking into account our other commitments, and we may wish to do more. There is an option to try that takes just a few minutes and may feel meaningful for us in addition to our prayers.

We sit in stillness with our feet on the floor, and become grounded and protected before opening the crown chakra. Breathe calmly and slowly, trying to breathe as slowly as possible but without any discomfort for a short while. Then imagine that, coming down through our crown chakra, a beautiful deep but bright violet light travels down through our head, shoulders, arms and into our cupped hands held in our laps where it forms a bubble of energy. Keep breathing slowly so that, when breathing in, the violet light comes in through the crown and, when breathing out, we are sending it travelling into our cupped hands. Continuously build this bubble of violet energy. It may be possible to sense this bubble of energy in our cupped hands pulsating as it grows in energy, as though we have north-north magnets pushing against each other.

After about six rounds of slow breathing we then imagine our family member, friend or pet in front of us, and we gently and slowly blow the bubble of violet light held in our cupped hands towards them, visualising them being showered in the violet light. Visualise the violet light gently travelling all the way down and around their bodies so that every part is bathed in violet light. When finished, we offer our thanks for their healing and then close down the crown chakra and become grounded in our chair once again.

Helpful tip: As the above entails working with our crown chakra, it may be best to hold a haematite crystal to aid with re-grounding ourselves afterwards. To help imagine the violet colour, use an amethyst crystal.

8th April – Feng Shui

For this month's Feng Shui tip we shall look at the Chinese Zodiac with its astrological animals of Rat, Ox, Tiger, Rabbit, Dragon, Snake, Horse, Sheep, Monkey, Rooster, Dog and Pig (also known as Boar). These animals, just like astrological sun signs, have characteristics and even within the animal sign there are five elements to consider in addition: wood, fire, earth, metal and water. So if we have worked out that we are a Monkey we may also work out that we are a Water Monkey.

The purpose of finding out our Chinese astrological animal is so that we can purchase a statue (or picture) and place it in a prominent position in our workplace. However, it is important to place this animal's position with respect; for example, a small statue of a dog could sit on our desk in an elevated position. This statue offers us the reminder of our characteristics so that we can work with our advantages but it also acts as a lucky talisman, always looking out for us.

As mentioned at the beginning of this book, the Chinese New Year alters slightly in its date between the end of January and the middle of February. People born around this time may need to refer to the animal of the previous year. For example, if you were born on 22nd January, 1952, the animal sign will be the Hare (which covers most of 1951). However, if born on 30th January, 1952, the animal sign will be the Dragon.

Visit your local library or search the Internet to find your own Chinese Zodiac animal and its element (search 'Chinese Zodiac' followed by your birth date).

Helpful tip: 'The Chinese Astrology Bible' by Derek Walters is user-friendly, helping us to understand the Chinese Zodiac. Taking this further, 'The Chinese Horoscopes Library' by Kwok Man-Ho provides further depth to the five elements for each animal.

10th April – Guerilla Gardening

This activity has grown throughout the world since the 1970s and is an activity for those living in towns and cities who love this planet and wish to help her in expressing her beauty, as well as growing useful plants that can be harvested such as herbs. There are many 'brown sites' and spare pockets of soil in our neighbourhoods where plants can grow and are perfect places for us to try some guerrilla gardening ourselves, to bring a little joy to our sometimes barren streets. These additional flowers, herbs, shrubs and trees planted by our guerrilla gardeners also help the native insects and bees.

Today, let's think about doing this ourselves by creating what's known as a 'seed bomb' with the specific aim of helping our bees. The following plants are of help all year long for the bees: rosemary, chives, thyme, lavender, spearmint, hellebore salvia, hebe, ivy, geranium, crocus, Michaelmas daisy, yarrow, cornflower, plantain, cowslips, meadow buttercup, sorrel and red and white campion.

Seeds can be obtained cheaply at a local garden centre. Our bombs are then created by mixing seeds with compost, sand and clay and with a little water. We mould them between the palms of our hands into balls and after a little drying time we then look for where to place our seed bomb: perhaps on a regular route we take to work or perhaps a small patch will be found at the end of the road where we live – then let the April showers do their work.

If we know several spaces where a seed bomb would brighten up our streets, then we can make several of them and bring a smile to light up our faces when we walk by them in the summer months, watching the bees tuck in to the pollen. How rewarding this would be.

Helpful tip: We could research and revive the ancient practice of 'tell it to the bees', which has become lost like so many of our countryside traditions. This may enable a closer connection with our bees, which very much need our help.

12th April – Beauty from Painful Emotions

As we follow our paths in life, we naturally accrue in our minds various emotions of a low vibrational energy such as annoyance, fear, jealousy and anger. If we ruminate too much on these they can affect our energy fields.

As humans on this planet we incarnate to learn, earn, work, grow, experience and gain wisdom; with all our experiences we naturally feel fear, annoyances and anger sometimes but it is important to declutter these from our mind, body and spirit. Similar to a spring clean of our homes, we also need a spring clean of our minds! Incidentally, this is linked with The Page of Wands in the Tarot, so if this particular card is drawn it is wise to pay attention to the emotions we hold in our minds and carry out a decluttering exercise for them.

One way to help relieve these thoughts and emotions from our minds is to try a Native American practice. Go into the country, find a secluded spot and dig a small hole in the ground. We then (if able to) lie flat on the ground and speak into the hole expressing all our angst and pain into the hole, ridding ourselves of any hold these emotions have on us. Afterwards we place in the hole a flowering bulb or several seeds, preferably indigenous to the area, and replace the earth over it. We thank Mother Earth for accepting our angst and request that the growing flower transforms our emotionally painful emotions into something of beauty.

Helpful tip: This can also be carried out on a secluded beach by planting some sea thrift or other fauna naturally growing along our coastline.

14th April – The Eye of Horus

The Eye of Horus is an ancient Egyptian symbol of protection and good health, being associated with royal power and the goddess Wadjet. We may recall old films set in ancient Egypt and notice an eye painted on the bows of ships; this was the Eye of Horus offering protection to the seafarers. Indeed, today in the Mediterranean we can still see the Eye of Horus painted on the bow of some boats in their picturesque harbours.

As the Eye of Horus was deemed a powerful amulet, let's research this further today, sourcing how it came into being through the ancient Egyptian legends and create this symbol ourselves by painting the Eye of Horus and placing it at the entrance to our homes as a form of protection for the home and all living in it. We could paint it on paper or on a flat pebble and place it in our homes, our cars or even in our boats.

16th April – Willow Month (15th April – 12th May)

Following the Ice Age in Britain, the willow tree was one of the first to regrow on the land and subsequently became a valuable resource for basketry and fencing through pollarding. To pollard a tree is to cut off the tops of the trees, enabling further growth, and thus becoming a sustainable resource. This is similar to the coppicing of hazel, although the cutting of hazel is carried out nearer to the ground. There are a few different types of willow: the crack willow is favoured by artists for charcoal drawing, cricket bats are made from willow, whilst the golden weeping willow can be seen in many large parks and gardens for their graceful beauty. And let's not forget that aspirin was derived from the bark of the willow.

Willows are often able to flourish along our river banks and do a great job of maintaining the riverside as their roots bind with the soil to help stop erosion. As willow is associated with water, on this day let us intend to drink more of the elixir of life, water. Hydrating our bodies is an absolute must for good health.

18th April – Angelica

The plant angelica, the stems of which are crystallised and used in baking, is also magically linked with angels. Some believe that angelica grown in the garden helps to invoke angelic light forces and beings. Today, we could consider creating an area in our garden where we can grow some angelica and sit in peace to meditate or think about angelic qualities that we would like to emulate. As we nurture and watch it flourish, we can allow it to continue reminding us to 'see as if through the eyes of angels' and behave towards others with caring and loving thoughts.

When we find these quiet moments to sit with angelica in our gardens or in a tub near our front door, we could try holding an angelite crystal as these are thought to assist in connecting with angelic energies. The colour of angelite ranges from a creamy white to light blue and a small tumble stone can easily be purchased at low cost from many crystal outlets.

Helpful tip: When planting angelica, bury an angelite crystal with it to help with further angelic connection.

20th April – Learn the Tarot

After watching the beautiful actress Jane Seymour using a Tarot deck in the James Bond film 'Live and Let Die', released in 1973, perhaps learning to use the Tarot seems a somewhat daunting prospect for many as the imagery of Tarot this film evoked was rather negative. However, this tool of divination used by many psychics and clairvoyants can be very informative for us if a challenge of some sort is pending or we would like some options to consider when we are feeling a little stuck.

Today, consider purchasing a Tarot deck and try working with it over a period of time to see what arises. There are hundreds of Tarot decks available and the vast selection on offer may be a little confusing, so it is important to take our time and choose a deck that resonates with us. If we have a love of animals, then source a Tarot deck with animal imagery, and the same as for angels. An important factor would be to seek one with good, clear imagery that can easily be remembered and therefore helps us to understand the main theme of the card drawn.

An easy reading to carry out is commonly known as 'What the Universe Wants You to Know'. It is a four-card reading and the first card drawn is linked with what we need to be aware of at the current time; the second card is associated with any challenges that may be linked with this; the third card offers an insight as to what could be helpful for us to consider; the fourth and final card is the outcome. This simple layout can be used when trying to make a decision about something or wondering why something occurred, enabling us to reflect on actions to be mindful of and actions that would be helpful, hence providing some thought-provoking moments hopefully to lead us forward.

Helpful tip: When learning the Tarot to give readings for others, perhaps to help raise funds at charity events, a helpful way to learn all of the 78 cards would be to list three or four words describing each card. Then we learn by rote, repeatedly reading these words through whilst holding each card in turn, looking at certain outlines and imagery within the card associated with the words. As proficiency grows, added phrases naturally wind their way into our terminology, often quite intuitively, and we find that we are able to recite a little story about each card. Thus we become ready to give readings without needing to refer to a book.

22nd April – Earth Day

Mother Earth, the Great Mother, the Great Goddess, Goddess Gaia, Pachamama and Mama Gaia are some of the names this planet is known by and she needs our help. The first Earth Day was on 22nd April, 1970. The organisers of Earth Day promote clean and green energy and concern themselves with environmental policies, climate change and the conservation of energy and water amongst other agendas. They rely on us to do our part in helping too. Let's research Earth Day now and discover whether we are able to take up any of the recommendations or activities to aid Mother Earth.

Perhaps organising a litter collection in our local community would be a fairly simple option that would really make a difference. Another way we can help is by researching and utilising renewable energy, as we are depleting much of the Earth's natural resources. Please let us do whatever we can to help our wonderful planet so that we can follow the well-known Native American phrase of "stepping lightly on the Earth". Renewable energy is sourced from sunlight, wind, tides, rain, waves and geothermal heat, not forgetting the sources for the production of biodiesel.

To get started perhaps the following websites may be of help: www.iea.org (the International Energy Agency), www.r-e-a.net (the Renewable Energy Association) and www.energysavingstrust.org.uk (the Energy Savings Trust).

On a spiritual level, we could also research the ancient Roman goddess Tellus. Goddess Tellus nurtured the growth of plants for our nutritional sustenance and during this period a festival was held by the Romans in her honour when people payed homage to her, petitioning her help and praying for the continuing health of the land and environment. It may be possible for us to plant a small fruiting tree in a large tub if we do not have a garden and call upon her to help the tree to grow with a plentiful supply of fruit. We may also wish to consider adding a figure of an Earth goddess at the foot of the tree.

The Earth goddess has been worshipped in many cultures from ancient times and is often represented as a kneeling or sitting female figure form with hands cupped holding a full belly, as from the Earth goddess all life is derived.

24th April – Painting Mother Earth

Two days ago we paid our practical attention to Mother Earth for Earth Day. Today, we could pay attention to her in an artistic way – and it doesn't matter what level of artistic talent we have. Find a sheet of paper and draw the Earth as viewed from space, perhaps with continents outlined in green and oceans painted blue, with the Arctic and Antarctic left white. Instead of painting stars around the Earth, paint pink hearts as if showering love and compassion onto her like falling rain. This picture can be elaborate or simple, multi-coloured or a pencil sketch.

Once this is done, light a pink candle near the picture and when doing so say a prayerful request for the candle flame to send its love and light to this beautiful planet. If there is time, perhaps a meditation visualising pink hearts falling as rain upon the planet and nurturing the land and oceans with its love and compassion could be carried out.

26th April – Playing Cards

Divination using cards is usually carried out with oracle and Tarot decks. However, our everyday playing cards can also be used and many psychics and clairvoyants used playing cards years ago when Tarot decks were not as popularly available as they are now.

Today, let's research this form of divination and see whether playing cards resonate with us better than the Tarot; after all, many of us remember handling playing cards from a young age and find the images of hearts, spades, diamonds, clubs and the court cards of Jack, Queen and King are comfortable to remember. Another thing in their favour is that the pack consists of only 52 cards and therefore somewhat easier than a full Tarot deck of 78 for committing their meanings to memory.

We may find that using the image of the ten of hearts on our vision board for a new love to enter our lives may help; perhaps the ten of diamonds, which predicts financial luck, is one we may wish to carry in our wallet. Have a little fun time today and check this out, especially as most of us will have a pack of playing cards somewhere in our homes.

28th April – The Hierophant in Tarot

In the Tarot, the major arcana card The Hierophant is linked with Taurus and with being tested by life's challenges. Today, let us reflect upon the challenges in our life and the mentor who has helped us through those tough times. They could have been a school teacher, a padre, a legal person, a member of our family, a nurse while we were in hospital or a supermarket cashier who just happened to say something we needed to hear at the time and provided a different perspective, empowering us to come through the other side of a difficulty.

Once we have our list, we sit quietly and express our grateful thanks for their support and interventions. While doing so we can also consider the times when we ourselves have acted as mentor for someone in need, perhaps quite unknowingly, and their response to us allowed us to understand that our empathy, thoughtfulness and kindness was all that was required.

Generally, we can be oblivious of the difficulties other people are working through when we go about our daily lives, as often their difficulties are private; when they are able to work with or meet kind and thoughtful people, this helps them in coping with their challenges. The Hierophant reminds us that we are all tested from time to time and therefore being mindful that our interactions come from a kind and gentle heart centre helps us all.

30th April – Walpurgis Night

Walpurgis Night in Germany is a gathering when witches come together to celebrate. This date is also Beltane Eve, a fire festival that denotes the renewal of life and rebuilding of the sun's energy. It is a time that reminds us to walk upon Mother Earth in friendship with all.

Today, let's sow some yellow flower seeds to represent the sun. The sun provides energy for us and at this time in the northern hemisphere we can feel it growing in warmth and energy. As such, the seeds we plant will represent our renewed energy for living and for building our plans. It is important to thank the universe and the spirits of nature looking after our flowers for their assistance in our plans coming to fruition; this can be achieved by pouring some holy well water or snow melt on the land as well as onto the seeds.

Helpful tip: Bury a sunstone crystal with the seeds. Sunstone's energy is joyful, nurturing and linked with luck.

May

What a beautiful month May is in our countryside with the hedgerows blooming in great array, the wonderful apple blossom in our orchards and wayside crab apple promising its fruitful harvest. Forays into the wild with foraging experts enables us to learn about using and working with free food. We can fully engage with Mother Earth's renewal and lush beauty.

May's moon is known as the Flower Moon, very apt at this time, with the fire festival Beltane, Mercuralia, the Feast of Pan and Helston Flora Day being celebrated this month.

2ⁿᵈ May – The Green Man and the Tree of Life

The rainforests of Mama Gaia help to maintain the natural balance of the planet's life force and are the lungs of the Earth. The Tree of Life is sacred in several cultures, known as Yggdrasil in the Norse traditions; the tree's roots reach down into the Earth whilst the leaves and branches reach up to the gods, with the trunk representing the middle ground of our present life on Earth in this incarnation. To some, trees represent transformation, fertility and stability and, when in full livery with their canopy of vegetation, the Green Man is clearly represented.

Carvings of the Green Man are found in old churches as well as remaining strong in pagan celebrations such as 'Jack in the Green' and is the leaf-covered man of the May festivals up and down the country at this time. There is a view that the Green Man is linked with Egypt's Osiris, the god of vegetation, and with Dionysus, the Greek god of the wild woodland. On this day, let's draw a picture of the Green Man by drawing oak, vine, hazel, hawthorn leaves, hawthorn berries and hazelnuts around a man's face. Better still, we may be able to collect some of these leaves and fix them as a collage to the overall picture.

Once completed, let us think about what we can do to help Mama Gaia, such as planting a sapling tree in our garden or growing a small ornamental tree in a large planter. Perhaps we can donate some of our time to planting trees in public areas as part of an action group. We may also be able to go for a walk in woodlands today or visit a church that has Green Man carvings; then sit in stillness for a while reflecting upon how religions and cultures are linked and ponder the one-ness of creation and its beauty.

4th May – Earthing

With Mama Gaia clearly showing evidence of lush growth and fertility at this time our thoughts naturally flow to being out in nature, whether working in our gardens, walking in the countryside or along our coastline as we notice a warming up of the air and soil. Planet Earth has an electromagnetic energy and it is believed that this energy can be felt through the soles of our feet when we place our bare feet on the land. What most of us tend to feel are tiny tingling sensations. Our feet are grounding tools for us in connecting to Mother Earth and what a perfect time today to research Earth Therapy, commonly known as 'Earthing'. We can try it for ourselves by sitting barefoot in our gardens, courtyards, on beaches or in woodlands and parks. The charge of energy we receive through our feet creates beneficial health changes for us.

The Lebanese philosopher and poet Khalil Gibran said, "And not forget that the Earth delights to feel your bare feet and the winds long to play with your hair." What a lovely picture this conjures in our minds.

In a Reflexology session, the therapist will massage various points on the feet, toes and ankles, which benefits the organs and structures of the body; so walking barefoot, when and where safe to do so, can become our own free Reflexology session! The different textures and undulations of the ground gently massage the soles of our feet as we walk along. Some venues even offer barefoot walking tours where special routes have been designed, taking us through waterways, mud and wooden walkways as well as the usual grass pathways, and this could be something that appeals as a fun group event to be organised if several friends wish to join in.

Helpful tip: Early morning grass with the dew still visible is a great time for Earthing. The book 'Earthing' written by Clinton Ober, Stephen T Sinatra and Martin Zucker, is recommended reading to help us understand this wellbeing activity.

6th May – Lavender, a Herb for May

Lavender is an incredibly versatile plant with many health-giving properties and benefits. Its aroma has a wonderfully calming effect and many use it as a sleep aid so being near lavender after a stressful day at work, or when we have a problem to consider, can help when we need to find a little calm oasis. Lavender is often used in magical charm work too for its healing power and bees also love this plant.

Another benefit of lavender is that its tight-budded flowers are believed to cleanse crystals and crystal jewellery, including silver and gold as they are also minerals. If we already grow lavender, then we can make plans today for harvesting, collecting the flower-heads and setting them to dry. Once dried, place the flower-heads in a glass jar and use these as a cleansing receptacle for any crystals after use. If we don't grow lavender already, let's buy a plant today in preparation; alternatively, dried lavender can be purchased in bags online or in crystal shops.

Helpful tip: If there is room in a section of our jewellery boxes, we could consider filling it with some dried lavender so that as we take off our necklaces, bracelets or rings, we can place them into the lavender and wear them again the following day knowing that they have been cleansing overnight.

8th May – Lily of the Valley, the May Flower

Lily of the Valley is included in bridal bouquets and mentioned in many poems, and it has brightened shady garden spots for centuries where its leaves provide good ground cover against weeds. Lily of the Valley is worn by the dancers at Helston Flora Day in Cornwall, which celebrates and welcomes the flourishing growth of the countryside and the early signs of the summer to come.

It is sometimes known as 'fairy cups' because fairies drink from its cup-like flowers, of course; however, we must be mindful that Lily of the Valley is poisonous to us! When blooming, this flower can also be known as 'the ladder to Heaven'. Lily of the Valley is also linked to the joyous Archangel Haniel, and when these delightful flowers are in a small vase with their green leaves in the background they certainly are a joyful sight to behold.

Today, let us spend a while thinking about the joys in our life, smile as we recollect them and allow that joyful smile to spread throughout the body. Even joyful memories from long ago can be rekindled to bring a smile. So we can lighten our day with joyfulness and invite Archangel Haniel to join us while doing so. Although there is room for much joy in our lives, as humans we can tend to dismiss many opportunities for joy to enter; so when we invite Archangel Haniel to join us, let's also request that we can start learning to recognise joyous moments better, and gradually increase these moments so they become part of our ongoing daily lives.

Helpful tip: Make a forward note in the diaries or calendar to plant some Lily of the Valley in the autumn, then we'll have some joyful reminders ready to flower the following May.

10th May – An Incense Stick

As the warmer days have usually arrived by this time of the year, we can take advantage by opening our windows and doors, if safe to do so, and allow the warm air to circulate around our homes. At the same time we could light an incense stick and set an intention for its smoke to cleanse and bless the home as it wafts around, being gently carried by the entering breeze.

There are many aromas available for incense sticks and some are created specifically with spell-work in mind. However, there are so many choices ranging from flower aromas to herb and spice aromas, not forgetting the very popular Nag Champa. Some have scary names such as Dragon's Blood, although this has a beautiful aroma and is favoured by many. Others may be named to inform us what they can be used for, such as protection, clearing and also certain meditation styles.

Today, let us source some incense sticks ready to light them regularly and allow them to waft through our homes on warm and balmy days over the coming months, being comforted that they will cleanse and bless our homes while doing so.

Helpful tip: Do experiment with whatever suits; some outlets offer the opportunity for free samples if we are undecided about a certain aroma and do not wish to purchase a whole pack.

12th May – Observing Animals

Observing the behaviour and actions of pets, whether our own or our friends', can make our routine interventions with them become much closer. This is not about making a formal study of animal behaviour, just simple observations of how our pets react to situations. The more we learn, the better care we are able to give them. Caring for others, whether human, animal, plant or the environment, can deepen our spiritual connection to Source.

We may observe a dog seemingly growling at nothing and we ignore their sign alerting us to something, then find we are late to respond to whatever the growling was all about. We may not see the visual triggers and assume there is nothing to be concerned about; however, dogs have much keener senses of hearing and smell than we do, with thousands more olfactory scent nerves for example, and can wind-scent or hear long before something enters our sphere.

How many of us have experienced for ourselves when watching a sad movie that our dog offers us a paw as they sense our emotions arising from the film? Perhaps our cats may curl up on our laps to sleep when we are experiencing a period of loneliness and they are just what we need at that time. Perhaps when in bed and feeling under the weather, our pets remain close by as if knowing that their company offers an uplifting support for us.

There are many enlightening and rewarding books on animal stories and their incredible connections with us and of course there are the marvellous guide dogs for those suffering sight loss, epilepsy or physical disability, as well as the PAT dogs (Pets As Therapy) that visit hospitals and nursing homes as company for the patients and residents. We must also not forget the wonderful horses that provide equine therapy, hugely rewarding for those in need who learn from the horses how to understand their own reactions in life. An example of this could be that if a veteran of the Armed Forces is struggling to move forward in civilian life and not trusting themselves, when given the lead rein to walk a horse alongside, the horse will more than likely not move forward as it senses the emotions, feelings and uncertainty being experienced by the veteran and reflects it back to them.

Love from a pet is a love that has no conditions. They do not append caveats to their love like humans can; it is a pure love for us. So let us honour and respect their love by deepening our connection to them and we may find that our own spiritual practices deepen further.

Helpful tip: If we do not have a pet ourselves, or a friend who has, perhaps reading a book on the subject will be rewarding. A good example may be the one written by James Bowen called 'A Street Cat Named Bob', which became a bestseller, of how a man and his cat found hope while living on the streets together.

14th May – Aloe Vera Healing

Aloe vera is a wonderful plant. It is believed that aloe magically brings luck and protection; however, it also has several beneficial health qualities, as evidenced by the many products on the market today. Simply snapping one of its succulent spikes will allow its healing sap to become available for immediate use – an example is that of an accidental burn in the kitchen from an oven tray and using aloe vera sap as a healing intervention. It is also possible to freeze this healing sap for use when required later. When using its soothing balm, it may feel good and comforting to know that we are able to use Mother Nature in her purest form to heal and nurture rather than an over-the-counter chemical remedy.

Today, let's investigate the healing qualities of this wonderful plant to see if it is suitable and appropriate for our own medicine cabinet at home. In any case, it makes a lovely house plant. When using this healing plant, don't forget to thank it for its healing energies.

Helpful tip: Bury a rose quartz crystal with the aloe vera to enhance its growth and plant health. An alternative to the plant itself would be to purchase a health drink containing aloe vera regularly, or healing gels made with aloe vera can be stored in our medicine cabinet ready for use.

16th May – Create Subject Folders

Magazines and journals are big business with millions being sold each week or month, many of us subscribing for them to be delivered to our homes regularly. However, what do we do with them after they've been read? Are they passed on to friends and family to share and eventually be recycled or are they stored in our homes, piling up in corners or scattered about, cluttering up our spare rooms or cupboards? Maybe we keep them because they contain articles we might want to access again – but this begs the question of how to find those precise articles at a later time. Moreover, if we store a pile of magazines at home, we restrict or block the flow of energy and this is not good Feng Shui practice.

Today, let's consider creating subject folders for the articles we have an interest in so that we can save the relevant information and then pass on the magazine or recycle it. Our folders could be ring binders, larger lever arch or box files, with dividers to maintain the different sections. Examples of sections might be meditation, crystals and healing, flower essences, healthy eating, interviews, science or massage and alternative treatments.

If we're planning to create a vision board, we could then cut out pictures that resonate with our desires and save them for potential use later.

Helpful tip: It may be useful to create a 'wildcard' section too, where the odd interesting article may be filed.

18th May – Paying Attention to the Universe

We all need nudges at times to motivate us into taking action. We may consider ourselves as generally well-motivated to do or start something; but what about being motivated to pursue a particular course of action that we had never thought about doing? Or perhaps we saw something and thought it sounded good… but then never took it any further?

There are times when it is wise to pay attention to continuous 'nudges from the universe'. An example of this could be when we notice an interesting advertisement in a magazine for some activity (say, a spiritual retreat) but we dismiss it, perhaps because of the financial commitment. Then we might see the same or a similar advertisement again later, and again. And then it comes once more in another magazine, this time with an attractive 'special deal'. We may wonder whether we had unconsciously sent a 'cosmic order' to the universe and now it is delivering; or was the universe making us sit up and pay attention to something that we needed to do? Whatever the activity, perhaps it has resonated with us because it is a stepping stone in helping us to achieve something important in our lives.

Something similar could occur with a specific book we would like to have but which has a hefty price tag; then after noting it on our radar several times, we find it by chance in a second-hand or charity shop.

From now on, let's decide never to ignore or dismiss what keeps arising for us, no matter what it is. It may be something we need to work on, it may be something we need to be aware of, it may be an activity we should take up as it will prove to be of benefit to us. Many think that these nudges are pure coincidence, but are we willing to let these coincidences fall by the wayside when they just might prove to be enlightening for us? Yes, it is important to be discerning about these potential opportunities and ensure that what we undertake is genuine. However, if we are not open to nudges from the universe, especially repeated ones, we could be missing something good.

20th May – Feng Shui

This month's Feng Shui quick fix involves the indoor succulent plant crassula ovata, commonly known as a jade plant or money tree. The jade plant can be rather plain to look at but can flower twice a year with dainty white flowers when they are happy in their spot. These plants are deemed to be auspicious and some homes have several dotted around, encouraging an abundance of good things into our lives. Some prefer to place their jade plant near the front door to welcome in abundance while others are specifically placed to coincide with the requirements of the room décor and directions of energy.

Today, why not buy a jade plant and place it near the entrance to the home, to invite and welcome in abundance energies? To add a boost to this energy, loosely tying an energising red ribbon around the main trunk of the plant will help.

Helpful tip: It is useful to know that the jade plant does not take to over-watering and it is probably best to err on the side of under-watering it.

22nd May – Ants

In 'Odd Days of Heaven', I wrote about spiders being our eight-legged friends but to try requesting that they do not enter our living space! Let's think about trying a similar request of ants today. Around this time of year we often encounter scout ants, which appear in odd places in our homes probably looking for a safe underground exit when the nest is ready to venture forth in the hotter months. If this happens, we can get an infestation of ants that makes us feel under attack from them, especially if they appear in several places at once. When they exit from their underground nests into our homes it can be quite a dramatic sight, with a shiny black moving mass of ants! So we usually get out the sprays, powders and gels to kill them and their nest, but it seems that no matter how often we carry this out they still return each year.

Instead of killing hundreds and possibly thousands of ants, which does not sit well with many of us, let's try making a request of the ants. It can work! So, when the first few scout ants appear, we trap them in a glass and let them know with our thoughts that they are not welcome in our homes, they are to return to the nest and inform the others to find their way into nature instead. State this to them with a real firmness of intent and then thank them in advance for remaining away. The trapped ant can then be released outside to take the message back to the nest. During the summer months, as ants are seen outside our homes on our steps or pathways, we can say our thanks to them again for remaining out of our homes as an added reinforcement of the request.

Helpful tip: Of course, there is a spell we could use! Mix dried sage (2 tbs) and mugwort (1 tspn) and place this in a black drawstring pouch. Set the intention for its purpose and then hang the pouch above the points where the ants are likely to enter our homes, such as a gap in the skirting board.

24th May – Becoming Attuned to Reiki

Reiki is not aligned to any specific spiritual practice or faith but is an energy healing modality, using that energy as a loving force for the highest and greatest good. There is a huge percentage of energy in the universe that scientists are unable to measure, called 'dark energy' because it is unknown. Some scientists now think that energy healers, such as Reiki practitioners and spiritual healers, are tapping into this dark energy and directing it for healing.

As well as being a healing modality, Reiki can help to fast-track our spiritual journey in certain ways; it certainly helps in the meditative practice of sending loving and healing thoughts and can increase compassion for ourselves and others. There are several Reiki systems to study, the original and simplest being *Usui Ryoho*, named after its modern founder, which has three levels of teaching: Level I is for channelling healing to oneself and close family or friends, Level II is for developing the practice as a business, and Level III is for Mastery, a deeper spiritual awareness. At each level there are 'attunements' given by one's teacher, simple rituals without which the energy healing doesn't seem to work, and one learns certain esoteric symbols for the mind to focus on in healing.

Over time, many Reiki practitioners find that they incorporate Reiki into their everyday lives and not just specifically for healing. For example, a Reiki symbol can be used for blessing food, water and plants; another Reiki symbol can be visualised when emergency services are called out or we see someone in trouble, offering extra protection.

Some alternative health practitioners such as massage therapists also offer Reiki and find that it enhances their massage. Reiki is about sending love, compassion and healing, and is a wonderful practice for us to consider studying.

26th May – The Lovers in Tarot

In the Tarot, The Lovers major arcana card is linked with Gemini and represents our choices and decisions in life. This is about considering the various paths open to us and what would be on offer along each path. One direction might offer a few opportunities but with a hard slog, another offers status but has little to distinguish it from our current life, while another path promises hard work but with the end result being a major and worthwhile achievement...

Today, we shall contemplate some decisions in our life, both major and minor. Did anyone or anything interfere with these decisions? Did we fully consider what we were committing ourselves to? Were our choices made with balanced thought? What were the potential opportunities of the paths presented to us?

When we think about the choices and decisions we have made, were some of them flawed due to a lack of information and therefore we weren't able to make balanced and wise choices? Perhaps the power-play of other people was a hindrance to us in some of our decisions and we found ourselves restricted. Were some decisions the best we have ever made in our lives, and if so why were they excellent? Sometimes, a good choice is to do absolutely nothing because stillness and patience are all that is required for certain situations to work through of their own accord.

These healthy reflections should help to empower us in dealing with choices and decisions in the future, having learned from considering aspects of our previous choices.

28th May – Dominoes Divination

Dominoes are often played by children but can continue to be played into adulthood, with league and social games offering much fun and companionship in pubs and clubs.

However, dominoes can also be used for divination. For example, 3 and 6 together means receiving a surprise gift whilst 2 with 6 means good luck in business or at work. If we have a vision board, then adding a domino to it to reflect some desire for our lives is an idea.

For manifesting, we may wish to place the 2-6 domino in the cash till of our business in order to increase sales. By far the 'best' domino is the 6-6 tile, which indicates happiness and success, so this tile could be placed in a prominent position in the home. If we hope to move to a new home, then perhaps the energy of the 5-5 domino will promote this as it indicates a happy house move.

Have a little fun today and check out dominoes divination, perhaps even buying a new set. There's always the fun, too, of playing this simple game with our family and friends.

Helpful tip: If buying a set for the home, it is best to purchase the thicker adult-sized tiles as children soon grow out of the small ones.

30th May – Forest Bathing

Much has been written about the benefits of the great outdoors, with vitamin D for our bodies from the sun and gardening helping to reduce depression. Connecting with nature can lead us to explore our moorlands, coastal regions and rolling hillsides. But today, how about visiting some woodlands, or a forest if we're lucky enough to live near one, and do what is known as 'forest bathing'.

In Japan, this is known as *shinrin-yoku* and they have an extensive range of special forest therapy trails throughout their country; it is considered a very worthwhile wellbeing activity, whether alone, with family or in groups. There are many beneficial effects recorded of forest bathing such as feeling significantly less anxious and having lowered blood pressure. Forest bathing has gradually extended to many countries throughout the world, where people can calmly contemplate while walking, practising mindfulness and absorbing the energies of the trees. Scientists advise that phytoncides emitted by the trees can aid our immune system; however, we may just sense a feeling of peace and a revival of the mind, body and spirit from this activity as we immerse ourselves in the energy of the place. Whilst in the forest we may wish to go barefoot to take advantage of 'Earthing' (see the 4th May entry).

When we visit a woodland we may wish to conduct a ritual of gratitude and respect for the trees, acknowledging various traditions throughout the ages, as trees represent spiritual growth and transformation. Many believe in tree spirits, known as dryads, and make an offering to them in gratitude for their energies by burying a crystal at the root of a tree. We could call upon Druantia, a Druid deity associated with forests, for assistance with a tree-hugging ceremony or with connecting to the energy of a particular tree.

In ancient woodlands or forests we may find ourselves in a sacred grove that was a place of worship in years past; we may only recognise this by sensing the energy of the trees and land at this particular spot. What a wonderful way to spend a day in late May, being with our trees which are usually all now out in full leaf with their vast array of greens gently swaying in the breeze. Such special places to be in.

If we need to collect wood in preparation for a bonfire, to celebrate midsummer next month or perhaps for our garden fire pit, then it would be respectful to consider where this wood has originated and to honour the fact that a living, growing tree has given of its life, or part of its energy, to provide this wood for our benefit. Maybe we have a wood burner to heat our homes in the colder months and continuously collect the fallen twigs and small branches to act as kindling that helps to light our hearth fires throughout the winter. While collecting the fallen debris, do we express our thanks to the surrounding trees for their bounty in helping to keep us warm during the winter? Mother Nature works in cycles and helps to nurture us, so respecting the trees and offering our gratitude to them for their part in this is proper. A simple way of doing this is to verbalise our sorrow at the tree losing some of its energy but also to thank it, stating that its purpose will be to provide us with warmth during the winter and that its old energy will not be wasted.

Helpful tip: A day spent with the trees may well create special memories and also enhance our spiritual journey, so that we would like to record this in a specific way. One possibility is to create what is known as a 'journey stick' where natural items found in the woods can be tied to a fallen tree stick, representing our journey that day. This journey stick will remind us of this time later at home.

June

This is the month of the summer solstice in the northern hemisphere and even though we may be busy, perhaps like the sun itself this month, let us pause for a few days and evaluate where we are with the resolutions we made at the beginning of the year. As we harvest the first of our herbs for drying perhaps we can reflect upon our own harvest of achievements and re-assert our plans for moving forwards.

The moon in June is known as the Strawberry Moon. Festivals taking place are the Summer Solstice (Litha), Golowan in Penzance, Fors Fortuna, Vestalia, the Feast of Hera and Sigurdsblot.

2nd June – Spiritual Art

Spiritual art is not only for gifted artists, it is for all of us to try and it's not necessary to have studied art formally to understand its qualities; we can simply work with what we feel is right for us and give it a go. We can create our own spiritual art with the usual paints, felt tips or crayons, and not forgetting the other mediums such as kiln glass work and clay modelling.

Perhaps we may feel drawn to certain spiritual symbols, such as the OM or other Sanskrit symbols, and wish to incorporate this as a relief on a small canvas by making the symbol from Polyfilla and painting it when dry. A simple but pleasant way of creating spiritual art is by using watercolour paint, or watered down acrylic paint, and scatter dollops of colour onto a sheet of paper which, with our eyes closed, we then allow to flow all over the paper as we pick the sheet up with two hands and move it up and down and in circles. We can often find that the abstract outlines created by this action 'speak' to us and we then take it further by perhaps adding glitter into the mix.

We may see, from the abstract outline produced, a tree with the energy of a dryad within the trunk or we may see the outline of a dragon…

Recognising that some of us do not feel able to draw outlines, we can use dots of varying sizes to create outlines which do not need to be definitive. These dots can be made with the tip of a fork (for example, use a plastic fork and break off the prongs leaving just the one to work with) and ranging to bigger sizes with the end of a pencil, going on to a bottle top.

If our artwork has produced a result we are delighted with, we could photograph it and produce copies to make personalised cards to give to our family and friends on special occasions. These could be complemented by spiritual poetry, prose or special prayers by peoples of the world, displayed in an artistic way.

Helpful tip: When preparing for a spiritual art session, a brief moment in stillness to connect with the inner spirit may be useful, or maybe a CD of Buddhist chanting will prove inspiring. Some may wish to pray for inspiration from an angel – this could be Archangel Jophiel (meaning beauty of God) as this archangel is said to assist the creative arts. Also, on a practical level, when using watercolours or acrylics, gently sprinkling table salt over the wet paint helps to create a textured effect when dry.

4th June – An Angel Altar

Angel altars are becoming more popular as we have become more comfortable in talking about angelic energies and our experiences with them in recent years. These altars can become focal points for our meditative prayer each day and be used as a healing bequest area by placing the name of someone beneath an angel figurine with a request for healing to be sent their way. For some, their angel altar is a physical outlet for building their relationship with angelic energies, to be sitting alongside when meditating and connecting with their guardian angels.

The creation of angel altars are personal to us. Whilst some may wish always to have flowers on display, others may prefer a small jasmine plant as this is associated with angelic energies. Candles can be included and perhaps even the odd white feather that arrived with us at a meaningful time. Crystals can be placed on angel altars and the soft blue colour of angelite is often favoured, or perhaps the striking green and white of seraphinite may be preferred. Selenite is another recognised crystal linked with angels. Of course, angel figurines are widely available nowadays, whether made from porcelain, wood or crystal, and perhaps a daily angel card may be placed on the altar in addition.

Today, let us spend a little time to considering the creation of an angel altar and where this can be situated. If family life is busy, this may be best on a shelf out of reach of young children. If we have a spare room for meditation, perhaps an angel altar would be best placed in here. Meditation time spent in peace and quiet induces a sense of gentle stillness for our mind, body and spirit and we may, during these times, have a sense of angelic connection.

Creating an angel altar is simple so let's give it a go and include any items that resonate with us as being angelic. There are no rules, just go with what feels right and enjoy the time spent in quiet contemplation alongside it.

6th June – Maneki-neko (The Beckoning Cat)

We are beginning to see more and more of this particular cat waving a paw at us from the windows of our High Street shops and eastern cuisine restaurants. The Japanese cat called *Maneki-neko* symbolises financial luck, depending upon which paw is waving. The left paw is believed to encourage customers into the shop or restaurant, whilst the right paw is associated with good luck and wealth.

The history surrounding *Maneki-neko* is a little unclear. One story tells of a Japanese shop owner generously feeding a stray cat near his premises and noticing that his finances had improved since the cat's arrival, with more customers entering his shop. Another story tells of a businessman sheltering under a tree during a storm opposite a temple where he noticed a cat using his paw as if beckoning him across to the temple. As the man moved forward, the tree suffered a lightning strike and he was saved.

Today, let us look into purchasing a *Maneki-neko*. If it is going to be placed in the home then find one with a waving right paw. If it is required for our business enterprise then a waving left paw may be more relevant. Also, a *Maneki-neko* cat may prove to be a perfect gift for someone whom we know to be in need of good fortune; they will value our thoughtfulness.

8ᵗʰ June – World Oceans Day

World Oceans Day was first officially recognised by the United Nations in 2009 although its grassroots phase concept grew in 1992. It has become extremely sad and distressing to see the news reports regarding the state of our oceans and the toll pollution is taking upon aquatic wildlife all over the world. As well as us relying upon the seas and oceans of the world for food and many other resources, they have an important climatic role. Yet we are destroying aquatic life.

However, it has also become heart-warming to note that many people the world over are actively doing something to help raise the profile of conservation work. Most encouraging is the engagement of the younger generation in understanding the consequence of plastic pollution and marine litter.

We can all play our part in World Oceans Day by joining in with a local beach clean-up, if we live near the coast, or visit an aquatic centre to learn about life in our seas and oceans and pass on this education to others. Perhaps we could make our own personal decision not to use plastic bags and containers anymore and to stop using beauty products that contain microplastic particles. We may wish to be part of a drive to make our own town or city plastic-free, having seen the new popular slogan 'Make (this town) fantastic and ditch the plastic'. If not near a coastline, perhaps we could liaise with local schools and suggest a special day trip activity with the schoolchildren, to undertake a beach clean-up. If truly land-locked, we could still take part in a river clean-up as most of our rivers eventually flow into the sea.

An important factor for World Oceans Day is that we pay attention to the pollution of our oceans not just on this special day but every day. Many people who regularly walk along a beach collect a few items of litter; but it would help if many more beach and riverside walkers followed this example and joined in picking up the litter each time the area is visited. Some areas have a voluntary code of picking up three articles of litter each time a visitor walks there.

Helpful tip: A good website resource for this day is www.world-oceansday.org.

10th June – Feng Shui

The colour red in the correct place is considered an excellent choice in Feng Shui and a good way to express this is with red geraniums growing each side of our front doorway; this is considered auspicious, helping to encourage abundance. It is important for the geranium plants to be healthy specimens; if they become spindly and look as though they are not flourishing at all, it is best to remove them and replace them with fresh and vibrant plants. Also, regularly dead-head the flowers as their energy wanes. Having a geranium plant on each side of our front doorway helps create balance which is also important in Feng Shui.

12th June – Protection on the Roads

Cycling is an extremely enjoyable activity, whether for competition, for getting to work or school, or purely as exercise. Biking holidays, where the whole family can take part, are also proving popular. Many consider cycling as a cost-effective solution for short journeys and it is recognised, especially as the population and number of cars grow, that there are important implications for climate change.

Unfortunately, all too often we see cyclists being overtaken far too closely and too fast by passing cars and lorries, and impatient behaviour by drivers when overtaking. Cyclists are vulnerable on our roads; they do not have a hard outer shell and any collision with a vehicle is potentially life-threatening. Therefore, whenever we see a cyclist travelling along the road from today, let's visualise Archangel Michael's shield around them as protection, or send a prayerful request to St Christopher, the patron saint of travellers, for their safety. If a family member or friend regularly cycles, then a small crystal to carry with them may help: some consider the combination of a moonstone and blue chalcedony to be a perfect choice for safe travel.

Helpful tip: During this month are two significant dates linked with cycling. There is World Bicycle Day on the 3rd June and also World Naked Bike Day on the 17th June. These could be researched for further information.

14th June – Sound Healing

Undergoing sound healing can be an incredibly cathartic experience for some of us and it is something to think about today. This therapy can be carried out with many instruments such as gongs, tuning forks, singing bowls (brass or crystal), Tibetan tingsha, the voice (known as toning), crystal bells and even the didgeridoo.

Pure sound carries a high vibrational energy able to clear stuck energies from our chakras and auric fields. South 'baths' often include a range of sounds that can gently penetrate our energy fields and offer a pleasing and soothing balm, having a knock-on relaxing and healing effect for our physical bodies. Some practitioners can help to bring about a subtle shift in certain chakra centres by creating sound for these specific areas.

For example, a practitioner working with tuning forks may feel that the area around a client's throat feels as though the instrument is circling through treacle. By working further on this area with sound, it may soon be found that the client feels better able to voice their concerns or say what needs to be expressed with compassion, whereas before they had felt uncomfortable doing so and had chosen to remain quiet, which led to the blockage in this chakra.

Today, let us look into sound healing and it benefits. There are several ways to experience sound healing and it is possible that a particular sound strongly resonates with us, such as a singing bowl.

Helpful tip: As singing bowls can be found in spiritual shops or at Mind Body Spirit festivals, it may be possible to try using one before purchase to check its resonance with us and how our bodies feel when the bowl is singing.

16th June – Releasing Emotional Negativity

We are human and all experience a huge range of thoughts and emotions each day. However, the more we hold on to any sad or stressful thoughts and emotions, the more they take hold in our energy fields. There are many opportunities for releasing these thoughts.

One handy way, when walking in the local woods, is to pick up a fallen leaf and transfer these thoughts to the leaf by holding it for a while and mentally visualising the thoughts travelling to the leaf like a marching army of black dots. If there is a stream in the woods, then stand near the stream, thank the leaf for accepting the thoughts and drop it into the water. Then thank the water for taking these thoughts away and cleansing them. The stream is helpful as water is linked with emotions, so using the energy of water to release emotional thoughts is part of the ritual. If there is no waterway, we can bury the leaf in the soil and thank Mother Earth for accepting our emotions, which she can then cleanse with her own nurturing energies.

Consider trying this from today whenever out walking near trees. We can sometimes experience a barrage of emotions in our daily lives, especially those who are empathic, and it is a simple practice to cultivate on a regular basis.

18ᵗʰ June – Jasmine Essence

As already mentioned, the heavenly scent of jasmine is said to attract angelic energies. Today let's try making a jasmine spritzer using mineral water or clear spring water in a jar. Place some jasmine flower-heads into the water for the day and leave it on a window-sill to soak up the sun's energy. Before the sun sets and the light fades, remove the flower-heads and decant the water into a spray bottle.

The next time we meditate, we can spray some of this jasmine essence onto our hands and gently waft this angelic flower essence around our energy fields, while doing so requesting our guardian angel to draw closer to us. We may wish to keep the jasmine essence spray near our angel altar and use it while meditating. We may also consider using it as a cleanser of the angel figurines on our angel altar.

Helpful tip: A word of caution: be mindful of the berries from the jasmine plant as these are poisonous!

20ᵗʰ June – Dice Divination

This is yet another old divinatory tool to pique our interest, using everyday objects. Most households have dice for use when playing board games; however, we can try using these today for divination. In olden times, a circle would be drawn in the earth or sand but today it is easier for us to draw a circle of approximately 7" (18 cm) diameter (the size of a small plate) on a sheet of paper. We shuffle three dice in our hands, quietly ask our question with eyes closed and throw the dice. The numbers on the upper side of the dice within the circle are added up and this number provides the answer to our question. For any dice falling outside the circle there are additional meanings: one die indicates difficulties arriving, two dice suggest a disagreement and if all three dice fall outside the circle then this is, surprisingly, rather lucky as it means wishes being fulfilled.

When adding up the numbers on the dice that fell within the circle, there is a great number of possible totals (some more likely than others). For example, 3 means sudden changes that will be to our liking, or a total of 16 indicates enjoyable travel. Of course, there are meanings that are not so good, such as 6 suggesting that finances are in trouble with a potential loss. Returning to a good theme, we have number 18 which forecasts luck and fortune.

Research dice divination today. When giving it a go, it's possible that quiet reflection on the answers leads us to realise that they were what we already knew in our hearts anyway. Divination is after all a tool allowing us to reach into our intuition and our unconscious mind, enabling thoughts, senses and feelings to be brought into the open. Dice divination is just one way of helping us. Happy casting!

Helpful tip: As with many activities enjoyed since ancient times, dice divination also has its superstitions attached, such as not carrying this out on a Monday. Similar to other divinatory methods, it is also best not to keep trying this several times during one day – or if we are not happy with the results!

22nd June – Moonstone, the Cancer Birthstone

One of the crystals associated with Cancer is moonstone; indeed, some crystal teachers believe that moonstone is Cancer's ruling crystal. There are several types of moonstone such as grey, peach, white, cat's eye and rainbow. Moonstone is a wonderful crystal to purchase for our life's journey and to work with when required. It can be used as a talisman and is good to hold when meditating for added psychic awareness. It can help women in their quest to connect with the feminine goddess within, and for men to find balance so their masculinity allows feminine aspects to be acknowledged and expressed as required, such as nurturing.

Like the moon's cycles, moonstone can encourage us to pay attention to our own cycles in life, allowing old ones to depart and new cycles to begin. They can be useful when specifically meditating to link with our higher selves in order to release old 'baggage' from our lives, as well as the residue of past lives. To help our ongoing journey intuitively, let's research and obtain a moonstone crystal today and enjoy working with it. A tumble moonstone is not expensive.

24th June – International Fairy Day

Childhood fascination with fairies remains for many adults – how delightful. These elemental energies help to look after our natural environment and there are people able to see, sense and link with these energies, often known as the Fae. If we research the famous Findhorn Foundation in Scotland, it is clear that the founders of this community in the 1960s believed that they were tapping into the interconnectedness of life and 'the intelligence of nature', collaborating with elemental life-forms. Several artists of fairies and the elemental realm have created fabulous pictures and many greetings cards seen in our High Street shops incorporate the Fae in their designs.

If we wish to attract fairies into our gardens, growing elecampane, primroses and bluebells is favourable. Consider allowing a wildflower area to grow in the garden too and have a little fun with creating some miniature fairy doors to place amongst the fauna, adding one or two miniature bells. Perhaps set a specific space aside with pretty stones and a water feature, also adding in a few fairy figurines. Occasionally, we may notice our pets responding to something unseen and perhaps this is the elemental energies being playful in our gardens with our pets as onlookers. If we do not have a garden, we may be able to 'adopt' a special place in a favourite park or woods, or there may be room outside our front door for some tubs in which plants can be grown and space made for the elementals.

Let us acknowledge the nature spirits today and bake some honey cakes so we can crumble some of them in our garden or by a tree for the Fae. Be happy today for this season in Mother Earth's cycle. Mother Earth shares her energies with us and so it would be a joyful action to pass this benevolence onwards; as the elementals look after our flora and fauna, then this is a way of expressing our gratitude to them. Maybe we are able to share some of the cakes with friends or work colleagues with joy in the giving, and put some in our children's lunchboxes for them to share and to learn the joy of giving to others. We can encourage children to be mindful of the Fae and to help to look after the countryside and the nature spirits. What wonderful memories these activities will evoke for them when reflecting back upon their childhood.

Helpful tip: Please grow the indigenous English variety of bluebells if planting these and not the continental variety, which can take over our natural bluebell habitats.

26th June – Dark Sky Sites

These sites are becoming popular destinations and continue to be recognised formally by local authorities as the artificial light pollution in our towns and cities increases. Those lucky enough to live in the countryside or near a coastline without light pollution may regularly make a date with certain stars and constellations and greet them like old friends, an activity that many town and city dwellers miss out on. At these recognised 'dark sky sites' we are able to stargaze and wonder at the beauty of the universe, enjoying ourselves by recognising particular stars making up the key constellations in our hemisphere during certain times of the year. They are also great places to visit when awaiting a specific meteor shower.

At this period of the year in the northern hemisphere, it is not until late in the evening that we are able to see our stars. However, this is a good time for us to seek out the dark sky sites and pay a visit during these warmer climes to carry out a reconnaissance so that we can plan for future visits when the darker evenings are with us again. Some of these officially recognised dark sky sites in the UK are listed below, but we can easily find others by getting out our maps.

South Downs National Park, Hampshire
Exmoor National Park, across Devon and Somerset
Kelling Heath, Norfolk
Stackpole Estate, Pembrokeshire, South Wales
Brecon Beacons National Park, South Wales
Snowdonia National Park, North Wales
North Yorkshire Moors National Park
Northumberland National Park
Galloway Forest Park, Dumfries & Galloway, Scotland
Coll, the Inner Hebrides
Shetland, the Northern Isles
Carrick-a-Rede and Oxford Island Natural Reserves, Northern Ireland

Some of the major meteor showers seen in the northern hemisphere on an annual basis are:

Quantratids (28th December to 12th January)
Perseids (23rd July to 12th August)
Geminids (6th to 18th December)
Ursids (17th to 25th December)

Each meteor shower has its peak time of appearing and we are usually notified on news channels of the expected event and the best time to see it during the night. There are, of course, several other meteor showers and we could perhaps research these too and make a plan to include these dates in our diaries so we do not miss out on their displays.

Helpful tip: Robert Dinwiddie's book entitled 'A Little Course in Astronomy' is a user-friendly book for the beginner or as a simple reference guide when visiting a dark sky site.

28th June – An Elderflower Sleep Cushion

The wonderful elderflower can be seen in our hedgerows at this time of year, with the promise of elderflower cordial and elderflower champagne being produced at home from its sweet-scented blossom. With artisan vodkas growing in popularity too, some prefer an elderflower cocktail made with vodka and champagne. The elder is a revered tree and helps us to understand the cycle of death and rebirth, honouring and respecting this cycle in all aspects of our lives.

Many people have periods of sleep problems and with the light evenings of summer and the occasional discomforting humidity, sleep can elude us even further. The greatly respected and versatile elder tree offers us, through its delicate flower-heads, an opportunity to create an elderflower sleep cushion by using the flower's relaxing energetic vibration. So pick an elderflower head today. After cutting, shake it to release any insects and then rinse gently in water. Dry it in a warm place for a short while and then place the flower-heads inside a pouch and leave this on the pillow for when we retire to bed. Sweet dreams.

Helpful tip: Approach the elder tree with respect and offer some holy water or snow melt in honouring its flowers being used for our benefit.

30th June – Continue to be Amazed

Many of us encounter such benevolence, kindness, serendipity and synchronicity in our lives that it feels amazing. Each time we ask for help or guidance from God, the Source, angels, guides, the universe or the spirit world, we can feel as though they never fail to assist us; we often say to others how amazed we are that we were helped once again.

Being amazed is part of our gratitude and respect for all we receive. If we relate this to Samuel Johnson's statement, "When one is tired of London, one is tired of life", we realise that if we were to stop being amazed by this world this could lead to our becoming ungracious towards its wonderful and mystical interventions, taking for granted all the help and guidance we receive. It is also possible, then, to lose our childlike innocence and wonder at the universe and the mysteries that await us.

So from today, let us never cease being amazed when our prayers and requests are answered and allow the ongoing amazement to inform and be part of our life's journey.

July

Picnics and general al fresco eating often begin this month with men taking over the reins of cooking meals with their (presumed) BBQ skills! Children look forward to the long school holidays with parents perhaps not so keen.

This month is the Hay Moon which is very relevant for the countryside. Festivals this month are the Feast of Cerridwen, Neptunalia and Feast of Sulis.

2ⁿᵈ July – Crystal Grids

A new way of crystal gridding that is gaining much popularity is that of using a small printed grid, incorporating sacred geometry. These are easily available to print at home and can be placed on our altar or perhaps on a shelf. There are many grids accessible: 'Metatron's Cube' may be preferred or 'The Tree of Life', but for many 'The Flower of Life' is favoured for its simplicity. The grids can be found online and in the clip art section of our computers.

When we have chosen and printed the grid we wish to work with, we place our crystals in a geometric pattern within the grid, starting with an 'amplifier' in the centre (clear quartz is a good one here) and then work from the centre outwards in a pattern. A crystal might be placed within each section; a Star of David outline or a simple spiral outwards may be preferable. When the grid has been staged, then we use a crystal wand to point at the central amplifier and set the intention for the grid's use, although a pointed finger is an alternative. Allow the grid to do its work but, if it is set for a long-term reason, then weekly cleansing will be required along with a renewal of its intention.

Examples of when to set a grid could be when wishing for more love and compassion in our lives, whether self-love or from others, and rose quartz would be the crystal of choice here. If a friend or family member is studying hard for exams then a grid of howlite may be appropriate. A grid of aventurine for when expecting hefty bills to arrive would be ideal as aventurine is a stone of prosperity and helps to draw in monies. We can use them for our pets as well, when a grid of aragonite or serpentine, or both, would be helpful. If desiring some peace in our lives then a grid of blue lace agate is ideal. Let us not forget about Mother Earth herself and set a grid of flint for healing this wonderful planet, whether as a general healing or if there is a specific disaster such as an oil spillage into an ocean.

Helpful tip: A book that greatly helps with understanding this form of crystal gridding is 'Earth Blessings' by Judy Hall. This book has a lot of focus on helping our planet; however, to know more about gridding for general everyday purposes then her book 'The Ultimate Guide to Crystal Grids' may be more suitable.

4th July – USA Independence Day

The 4th of July is probably the most famous Independence Day of countries throughout the world. Independence represents the growing pains of nations governing themselves and being free of controlling regimes and strictures of the past.

Today, let's light a candle and say a prayer for all those nations that have achieved or are seeking independence, so that their actions and governance are guided by honourable and compassionate intentions. Let us include in our prayers our applause for their efforts as beacons of light for other countries and peoples throughout the world.

6th July – Upcycling

It is commonly understood that we cannot keep going at our current rate of landfill for our domestic rubbish and recycling has become the norm for many people. We can donate our items to charity for re-use and re-sale, which is of great help. However, how about trying to 'upcycle' some of our items at home?

Perhaps we have an old kitchen table and chairs set which no longer suits our new décor, yet painting or re-staining in another colour may give the dining set a new lease of life. Or perhaps we may have some wall art where the original colours have faded and our first thought is to throw away this jaded item; but sometimes there is nothing like the element of gold to imbue a new energy. An example of this is the picture for July, where the Buddha face wall art has been painted with a creamy yellow base and over-sponged with gold, providing a richer effect. When we upcycle our once-beloved items, they can again become much-loved favourites, either for ourselves or as gifts for others.

From today, let's consider the option of upcycling our furniture or other items so that we can do our little bit to 'tread lightly'.

8th July – Holly Month (8th July – 5th August)

The holly tree is linked with the Druids and 'rules' the dark half of the year. It is associated with death, rebirth and renewal as well as with protection. This part of the cycle of the year is a time to celebrate our achievements, perhaps having worked hard in recent months on the projects we planned at the start of the year.

To celebrate our achievements, today we could make a dessert of red berries such as raspberries, cherries and strawberries (these will represent holly berries). We then take two bowls of melted chocolate, one of white chocolate (representing the light half of the year) and the other of dark chocolate (representing the dark half). Individually dip each berry into one of the chocolate bowls and place them on a tray, allowing them to solidify ready for eating.

As we eat them, for each chocolate-covered berry we verbally state our acknowledgement of what we have achieved thus far. If this is carried out with our family, then each member in turn makes their own acknowledgement. We often do not allow ourselves the luxury of verbalising what we have achieved in our lives, tending to remain quiet, so let this be a time when we allow our voices to be heard. The Four of Pentacles in the Tarot is associated with us not fully recognising our achievements and reminds us to think more kindly of ourselves. So if we have a Tarot deck, this card could be placed on the table. If we conduct this ritual with family, we should also congratulate one another on the achievements as they are listed one by one. After all the chocolate berries have been eaten, we should feel a little more uplifted and satisfied with our achievements due to the kindness expressed to ourselves and others.

Helpful tip: A simple alternative to the above is to use white marshmallow sweets, half of which are dipped in dark (or milk) chocolate.

10th July – A Crystal Workshop

Crystals are loved the world over and many of us learn how to use them from books and online courses. They are desired and used for many reasons, such as in beautiful jewellery, alongside vibrational healing for humans, animals and plants, with meditation, on our altars and for charm work, protection, gridding and gifts, to name but a few. There is so much to learn about these wonderful stones and although the many books available offer guidance, a workshop with a crystal healer or teacher can hugely enrich the process.

Today, consider attending a crystal workshop taking place in our locality where, after learning the theory of some crystals with their individual energies and how to use them for specific purposes, we shall also be able to practise the theory. The crystal healer or teacher being present at all times and continually guiding us is valuable for our learning and aids our ongoing relationship with these powerhouses of energy. There is so much to be gained from crystals so why not go ahead, give it a try and see if a crystal workshop is suitable for us. If we find it enjoyable then learning about and understanding crystals might become an ongoing hobby.

12th July – A Healing Altar

Like an angel altar, this can be created in whichever way resonates with us. We may prefer it to be on a shelf or on an occasional table located in our meditation space; or, in following Feng Shui, we may create this altar in the spiritual centre of our home. We may wish to add photographs of loved ones who are unwell, along with various crystals and figurines to represent people and animals. We could add written healing prayers that are meaningful to us or spiritual verse that has a healing content. We may like to add pictures and icons from different faiths such as Quan Yin, St Francis of Assisi or even a snake (to represent the healing caduceus). Many people keep a book on their healing altar that contains the names of people for absent healing.

Some Reiki practitioners use an animal figurine as a surrogate and paint various Reiki healing symbols on it. The Giza pyramid shape has long been considered special too and many crystal therapists will place a photograph or person's name under a crystal pyramid with the intention for healing. Serpentine is linked with nature and helps with sending distant healing and is perhaps a good crystal to be considered for our healing altars. Some people like to have an icon of the Madonna and Child and underneath this place the name of family or friends who are expecting a baby.

As we walk past our healing altar many times each day, we should think of the healing for those in need and even this simple acknowledgment is a compassionate energy sent out into the universe. Today, let us consider creating our own healing altar and place on it those items that resonate with us. When passing by, it helps to focus our healing thoughts for those in need even if only for a short moment.

14th July – A Rose Room Spray

How gorgeous are roses, whether those grown for their perfume or for their beauty. There are many special connections with roses; they are symbols of love and martyrdom and are linked with the Norse goddess Freya. The colours of the roses have further meanings: red for passionate love, deep pink for unconditional love, pale pink for romantic love and white for pure love.

Today, let's make a spritzer with rose petals. Choose roses with the colour and perfume that suit our desires. Shake them so that any insects can fly free and one by one place each petal in a glass jar, then pour mineral or spring water, or snow melt, to the top. Seal the jar and place it outside on a windowsill to soak up the sun's energy. After a few hours, decant the liquid only into a spray container ready for use to spritz our rooms or linen cupboards.

Helpful tip: When cutting the roses don't forget to thank the plant and flower for their wonderful energies and acknowledge that they will be used for a good purpose.

16th July – Switchwords

Our words are powerful, hence the well-known phrase, 'the pen is mightier than the sword'. Some believe that the words we voice create an energetic vibration that can affect the meridians in our bodies. In traditional Chinese medicine the meridians and certain acupressure or acupuncture points running throughout our bodies are worked on to aid our health and wellbeing. As there are also meridians within our mouths, it's clear that when we speak words of a low vibration (e.g. gossiping, swearing or blaspheming) we can detrimentally affect the wellbeing of a meridian as it flows throughout our body, possibly affecting other areas. So, by speaking words of a higher vibration (i.e. love, compassion and kindness) we can help to maintain healthy meridians.

Liz Dean, the author of 'Switchwords: how to use one word to get what you want', offers her user-friendly book to enable us to understand how one word, or a short phrase of, say, three words said together, can help us in a form of affirmative cosmic ordering. As the switchwords she recommends are helpful and encouraging, and can assist us in improving or changing our behaviours, then the vibration of these voiced words can have a positive effect on our meridians too. A popular three-part switchword she recommends is "angel-thanks-divine", which is a way of expressing our gratitude to the angels for the help they provide to us.

Today, consider buying this book if we believe it will be useful.

Helpful tip: We could also search the internet to learn about James T Mangan, an American who created what is known as 'The Universal Switchwords List' in the 1960s.

18th July – Reflexology

Reflexology is an ancient practice that has become very popular in modern times and many consider this regular complementary therapy a mainstay of their body's wellbeing. For those who are not able to allow their feet to be touched, as they are highly sensitive (or extremely ticklish!), the opportunity for Reflexology need not be missed as it can also be carried out on our hands. The organs in our body are reflected in certain areas of our feet, likewise our hands, and by massaging certain areas or exerting a little pressure we are able to promote our body's wellbeing. The techniques used help to trigger various responses throughout our bodies, such as relaxation.

It is possible to learn a few little Reflexology practices ourselves to use as a quick-fix for, say, a headache where we feel the pain in our head, face and sinus areas; we can manipulate the dorsal of our thumb, just below the nail, with short stroking pressure from left to right across the thumb to bring about some relief.

Today, let's check out Reflexology and perhaps enjoy many evenings of self-massage.

Helpful tip: Many MBS Fayres offer taster sessions of various healing and therapy modalities and trying Reflexology at one of these may be a good opportunity for deciding whether to adopt this as a continuing complementary practice for our wellbeing.

20th July – Feng Shui

Bamboo is a very versatile plant with many uses following its harvesting. In Feng Shui, bamboo is regarded as an auspicious plant and many like to see it growing healthily in their gardens as it represents abundance. Some prefer the bamboo to grow in the east of the garden as this is considered good for the health of the family.

There are several varieties of bamboo easily sourced at our garden centres, so today let's consider purchasing bamboo to grow, whether in a large tub outside our door or perhaps a taller variety if our gardens are large enough and there is a particular area for it to thrive.

Helpful tip: A word of caution if growing bamboo in the garden – it easily spreads and can take over a large area if not kept under control. (I said it was associated with abundance!)

22nd July – Pay it Forward

This is a kindness action has been around for many years, in which we anonymously pay in advance for the next person in the queue behind us, such as for a cup of coffee or a newspaper. In a similar vein, perhaps some of us may have previously helped a customer at a till by paying for an item of grocery they did not have quite enough money for. This energy of kindness can be contagious with the recipients also adopting this action later, having experiencing the kindness for themselves.

Another way of paying it forward but with the potential for an added surprise is to pay for a raffle or tombola ticket for the next person. Just think of the extra special joy we would sense in our bodies if their ticket was drawn, especially if it was a child and their exuberance at winning created great happiness. From today, we could try adopting this practice at fetes or other events whenever we purchase a raffle ticket for ourselves, by buying an extra one to be given to the next person.

Helpful tip: It is important for this kind action to be made anonymously in order to avoid any awkwardness of feelings should the winning recipient be made aware of the donor.

24th July – Strength in Tarot

In the Tarot, the major arcana card of Strength is associated with the astrological sign of Leo and is often depicted as a spiritual warrior, male or female, battling a lion and holding the lion's head or mouth. This card reminds us about having the spiritual strength to succeed and overcome challenges in our everyday lives and encourages us to request support from our spiritual allies in our quest to reach the light at the end of the tunnel.

A great spiritual strength is that of having empathy, love and compassion for all things, including ourselves. If we are able to recognise these spiritual strengths within us, perhaps today think of any challenges we faced and how we overcame them. Did love, empathy and compassion play their part and if so did we sail through the difficult time in comparison to how others fared? It often requires courage to incorporate these spiritual strengths into our way of life so they become second nature. If we consider that our spirits are full of love, empathy and compassion that can occasionally become imprisoned behind bars due to our everyday fears, it requires strength and courage for us to break down these bars of self-imposed protection.

If after reflection it is felt that we require this strength, then we can ask for help from the spirit world and our higher self to guide us. This can be done with a simple prayerful request, whether according to our own belief system or by simply requesting the universe for its assistance.

Helpful tip: Holding a rose quartz crystal for its compassionate love energies may help in any reflection. If wishing to light a candle, perhaps one pink and one red candle will help; the pink is for compassionate love but the red is to offer the vibrant energy of courage, strength and passion needed to break free.

26ᵗʰ July – IT Detox

Many parents set limits on their children's access to television, the Internet and gaming in terms of the time spent on these activities. However, with mobile `phones prevalent in our society it has become difficult to set these limits as it is the norm to be able to access so much information and activities now. But what about our own behaviours in terms of IT, when so many of us use our mobile `phones as if they were appendages to our bodies? There is much information now regarding the detrimental health issues associated with this technology, such as the blue light emitted having an impact upon the melatonin being produced in our bodies, and their electromagnetic fields affecting the brain.

IT has permeated our workplaces and computers have become the workhorses of the day, so it is difficult for us to carry out a detox in our work environment. But then on arriving home, many of us access our social media pages, our emails as well as general 'phone calls and texts, not forgetting our surfing of the Internet. We can become bombarded with information and occasionally it is pertinent to question the validity, and the quality, of the information.

From today, let's try to find a little more balance in our lives from all this information technology in whichever way it is communicated, and make some space away from it, by simply sitting in peace or having a family supper where we can enjoy conversation face to face. A way to achieve this is to try one hour each week initially and gradually work up to an hour each day. Perhaps this time away from IT can then be stretched to two hours each time we set our detox.

We may find that our family dynamics improve as we are able to offer quality time to one another, and our everyday lives become enriched as we are able to pursue other activities. A good time to start this is at the beginning of the school summer holidays. Maybe we are also on holiday at this time and only need to access IT at certain times, so this would be a good starting point.

Helpful tip: It may be relevant for us to set some boundaries with our family and friends when letting them know about our IT detox, as they may not understand why their joking texts sent at midnight are not being responded to! This can be achieved by simply letting them know of our intentions so they are not offended when we are slow to respond.

28th July – Smudging Sticks

Sage grown in our gardens for culinary purposes offers a pleasing aroma as we pass by and touch its leaves, often wafting the air around and deeply breathing in the perfume left on our hands. Sage has also been grown for its herbal and medicinal healing qualities, often seen in the physic gardens of monasteries. White sage is grown for the specific purpose of spiritually cleansing our homes, altars, spiritual tools, crystals and ourselves as we waft it around our energy fields.

Smudging sticks are easy to make. It's not necessary to create the thick bundles purchased in shops as we can cut just three sage stems to make a smudging stick for our own use at home. To make these, in the late morning (allowing for dew to have dried and for the energy of the plant to be vibrant in the sun) we first respect and thank the sage plant for providing us with its energy. We then cut the sage stem at approximately 10" (25 cm). Have some good cotton ready and tie three stems of the sage with the cotton as an anchor. Then fold the sage stems in half so that the top half doubles back to where we tied the cotton, and start to wrap the cotton around the folded over stems. Usually a criss-cross patterning with the cotton is preferable, returning to the original starting point. Once completed, the smudging sticks can be placed in a wicker basket or hung in a warm place such as an airing cupboard until dried, after which they can be stored in our spiritual store cupboards ready for when required.

Helpful tip: Making a gift of home-made smudging sticks is an option to consider for our friends, especially if given in pretty home-made packaging. Maybe incorporate the petals of rose flowers to make the smudge stick colourfully appealing.

30ᵗʰ July – A Healing Meditation

There are hundreds of meditations for healing as we can create in our minds whatever we wish to occur for healing, whether for ourselves, family, friends, animals or the land and nature. Many people have their own favourite that feels comfortable for them. A popular one is below, so if not having done a healing meditation before we might try this today.

We prepare ourselves for meditation and sit in a chair or on the floor for grounding and protecting ourselves. When ready, imagine the heart centre opening as if a rose flower and a little fibre-optic tendril coming out of the rose and travelling to the centre of the room. When it reaches the centre, a pillar of bright light comes down from the divine universe and carries on into the ground through the fibre-optic tendril. Within the bright light of this pillar, imagine seeing rays of gold, silver and bronze with flecks of violet all swirling and flowing together to form a beautiful sight. We then visualise within the pillar those whom we wish to receive healing.

Imagine them glowing in the bright light, surrounded and comforted by the gold, silver, bronze and violet falling upon and around them, caressing and soothing their bodies. Imagine those we have placed within the pillar looking a picture of health and see them happy and smiling. For those who believe in angelic energy, perhaps imagine angels surrounding them.

When it's time to close the meditation, visualise them waving as they gradually fade from view. The pillar of light can return up to the divine universe and we allow the fibre-optic tendril to return to the rose in our heart centres; then we close down this chakra by closing the rose into a bud and placing a golden disc of light over it.

It may eventually be noticed, if we carry out this meditation on a regular basis in a particular room, that where we imagine the pillar of healing light to enter there seems to be a feeling of warmth. When this does occur, some believe that the warmth is a reflection of the source of divine love and healing we have created in our meditations, which then lingers. So try giving this meditation a chance today. Also, around this time is the International Day of Friendship so we could extend this to include our many friends throughout the world to reflect the interconnectedness of life.

August

This month of busy outdoor activities with children, followed by relaxation during balmy evenings, offer us many good memories. We may gather with our families and friends making for large groups as we assemble in parks and at beaches on holiday. Lazy cricket games are played and children swap contact details as each get-together finishes and our homes beckon us once again.

The moon this month is the Barley Moon, quite apt as this reflects the first of the harvests. Festivals during August are Lammas (or Lughnasah), Raksha Bandhan, Freyfaxi and the Festival of Torches for Nemoralia.

2nd August – Painting Pebbles and Stones

With the summer well and truly with us now and the schools and colleges closed for the holidays, we are often out and about whether on our own or with our partners and families, perhaps spending time at the beach, lakeside or riverside. At these locations, pebbles abound and many of them attract us into picking them up to look more closely at them. If on holiday, we may wish to take a few home as mementos of an enjoyable time. Today, we could think about searching out pebbles that we will be able to decorate and take them home with us in preparation. If we have a young family, this activity can entertain children for many hours. There are several ways of decorating pebbles and below are some ideas to be considered.

Unusually shaped pebbles and stones can be sought, such as those looking like a number; we may live at 'number six' and find a stone that resembles the outline of 6, then we could paint this number on the stone and place it by our doorway. Perhaps we spot one with an outline of the face of a Disney character and decide to paint this on the stone. Be open to what enters the mind when we see an unusual shape; pick it up and observe it from all angles and allow ourselves the freedom to visualise various possibilities.

Another option is to find small flat-sided pebbles on which we can write words such as 'gratitude'. These can be our gratitude stones that we can place in our homes or workplaces, or give to our family and friends. If running a business then placing a gratitude stone in the cash box sparks the high-vibrational energetic thought of gratitude within us. Alongside the word we can incorporate an easy pattern or simple flower in order to pretty it up a little. We don't have to be concerned about our artistry and just make the word pretty in various shades of colour, following our instincts.

We can also consider writing other uplifting words such as love, compassion, joy, trust, renewal, happiness, play, peace, kindness, serendipity, abundance, transform, inspire, strength, cooperate, serenity, balance, charity, health and beauty. After painting the pebbles we can place them in a pouch and use them as an oracle, pulling one out each day so that we can focus on the word and its full meaning, allowing it to play an active part in our lives.

We could also use larger flat-sided pebbles or stones for painting patterns upon. Perhaps we may love the ancient Celtic spirals, columns and knots, and find some perfect stones to try these out. We may find some circular-shaped stones and paint a mandala, or maybe we just paint what children often do, whatever is felt in their hearts. Indeed, if we're with children when carrying out this activity, we could just follow what they decide to paint; they may well come up with fairies, angels, mermaids, unicorns and dragons and what lovely pictures we can create from these.

A more unusual option to be considered if a family, friend or work colleague is suffering from an illness, is that of seeking out a larger stone and on one side paint an uplifting phrase such as, "May the long-time sun shine upon you"; then decorate this side of the stone with a few spirals or circles around the phrase. On the reverse side, arrange for family members, friends or work colleagues to sign their name in an indelible marker and give this as a way of offering our loving support to them during their illness. This gesture will probably be highly valued by them and be placed it in a prominent position in their home.

Helpful tip: A layer of varnish over the painted pebbles will help to maintain them and if decorating a stone with, say, angels and unicorns, then glitter glue will dry with a protective texture as well as providing a bright colour.

4th August – Giant Thanks

We express our gratitude in many ways, whether to a person for their actions, writing in a gratitude journal or maybe as a silent prayer of thanks to angels when a desired outcome has been achieved. However, let's make a giant thank you statement for the universe today!

The easiest way to do this is by using a stick and writing 'thank you' in the sand of a beach in giant letters. If the beach does not have wet sand where it is easy to draw, instead try creating these two giant words with stones, and if unable to visit a beach then perhaps a lakeside or riverside will be more suitable. This is a loving and grateful energy being sent out to the universe and when others see this giant thanks written in the sand it may encourage them to reflect on how often they do – or do not – express gratitude themselves. Perhaps our giant 'thank you' may help to change this.

Helpful tip: After writing 'thank you' we could add the small outline of a heart.

6th August – Past Life Regression

This is usually offered as part of a hypnotherapy session. But there have been instances when people have spontaneously reverted to a previous lifetime – as though seeing things around them from two hundred years ago and instead of seeing cars travelling along the road they see coaches and horses – and all without the aid of hypnotherapy. Some may wonder whether this was their imagination; then a couple of years later an incident might occur, or something is said, and the experience of past life regression is brought to mind again.

Novels have been written about similar instances, such as Daphne du Maurier's 'The House on the Strand' and the more recent 'Outlander' series by Diana Gabaldon. An autobiographical account written by A I

Kaymen entitled 'Aura Child' is a fascinating read, encouraging us to change our perspective of how others see the world we live in.

Some wish to research the history of the images and insights gained from their regression and enjoy delving into names, dates and records in order to help them gain further understanding of their past life during that era. One author who did this was Sarah Truman, making the surprising discovery that she had almost certainly murdered her present-day partner in the eighteenth century! Her story is told in 'Haunted by Past Lives'.

Seeking a past life regression session may be due to a desire to understand an irrational fear one has, a fear that has no basis in any events during our current life. There is no guarantee the regression will shed any light on this immediately, but it may become clearer in time. For example, being afraid of being on a beach at night might have the explanation that in a past life we drowned close to a beach when a ship went aground on rocks during the night. This very traumatic memory holds an energy that can be carried forward into our next life – and sometimes into several lives if we do not work on this memory to clear it from our energetic make-up.

As many believe we incarnate to experience, learn and grow, then allowing these fears and phobias from serious events in previous lives to form a block can prevent us from moving forward in our current lives. These blocks may even present as an all-consuming fixation for us and jeopardises our potential for living a fulfilling life.

Today, we could research past life regression to learn about this subject. If we have an irrational fear, phobia or reaction that affects us badly then perhaps a past life regression with a hypnotherapist may be an option.

Helpful tip: Sylvia Browne's book 'Past Lives, Future Healing' is a very informative read and Dr Michael Newton's classic book 'The Journey of Souls' could also be of interest.

8th August – Feng Shui

The Chinese requested that their Olympic Games should start on the eighth day of the eighth month in 2008. The number eight is extremely auspicious in Feng Shui and in play here is 'the power of three'. The tip for this eighth month is to purchase what is known as 'a wealth toad' and place it in the entranceway of our home as if welcoming wealthy abundance into our lives. The wealth toad has three legs and a Chinese coin held in its mouth, while sitting on several other coins.

The wealth toad faces the door; however, some Feng Shui experts advise that at night it should be turned away from the door and the coin removed, in order to provide the toad with rest before starting its work again the following morning when we replace the coin and face it towards the front door once again.

10th August – A Feather Holder

Last month we prepared some sage sticks for us to use in spiritually cleansing our homes and our bodies, and now it's time to create a holder for feathers so we can waft around the cleansing smoke. Some prefer to use one meaningful feather, such as from an owl, and some are lucky to have an eagle feather. A decorative leather cord can be tied around the end for comfortable holding. However, we could produce one similar to that shown at the start of August, especially if only able to access the more common feathers.

We collect the feathers we wish to use; for the example picture, these are a mixture of swan and seagull feathers. These are water birds and, as water is linked with our emotions and especially for those who are empathic to the energies of others, this may be a good choice for wafting the sage smoke around our bodies. Of course, shells are linked with water too, so obtain shells like the scallops shown, which can be purchased from fishmongers, and give them a good clean before painting them in any way desired. When dry, add Polyfilla sandwiched between the two shells and then pierce the Polyfilla with the feathers to form a fan display. We then allow it to dry fully, which takes a couple of days.

Whether we make these decorative feather holders for ourselves or give them to our friends, this is a simple creative task made with thought, time and attention so they can be very meaningful to us.

12th August – The Perseids Meteor Shower

This meteor shower runs between approximately 23rd July to 22nd August each year in the northern hemisphere and the peak date recommended for viewing it is the 12th August, when up to a maximum of eighty meteors can be seen in an hour. On this night, dress appropriately with warm clothing handy (usually by now any balmy weather does not remain late into the evening) and sit outside in a comfortable seat to look out for the meteors. With each meteor seen we can express forgiveness of ourselves for various incidents throughout our lives. We may recall cringing moments wishing we had never said or done something! There may be momentary thoughts of strong emotions such as anger and jealousy towards family and friends that we prefer not to have occurred.

These thoughts and feelings can form low vibrational emotional patterns in our energy fields so this is an ideal opportunity to forgive ourselves. If after a while we are also ready to express forgiveness towards those whom we feel have caused us harm or a disservice, then we can move on to forgiving them with each meteor viewed. Spiritual teachers tell us that forgiveness of others allows the negativity to be released from our hearts and for a higher power to accept them, thus enabling us to become free. If the heart is a window that has become smeared due to negative emotions, then how can the Light shine through to help us in our healing and enable us to move forward?

Ho'oponopono (a Hawaiian ritual) may be tried during this meteor shower for forgiveness by using its phrases, "Thank you. I love you. I am sorry. Please forgive me. Help me. Show me the way. I am ready. How can I serve?" When we link this eight phrase *Ho'oponopono* to the usual eight points in a tapping round (the Emotional Freedom Technique), we may find this helps us further and makes the session a very meaningful event. When a memory comes to mind that we wish to release, we can voice and tap like this:

Eyebrow	"Thank you for bringing this memory to mind."
Side of eye	"I love you."
Under eye	"I am sorry this memory is emotionally hurtful."
Under nose	"Please forgive me for holding on to this memory."
Chin	"Please help me to release this from my mind, body and spirit."
Collarbone	"Please show me the way forward."
Under arm	"I am ready to move forward."
Crown of head	"How can I serve?"

When we say these phrases, we are speaking to our inner child, our soul, our higher selves; the phrases are not being directed at another person. Shamanic teachings encourage us to understand the interconnectedness of life and, by working on ourselves to bring about a change in our harmonic energy with forgiveness, this can also naturally bring about a change in others.

Tapping can be a very dynamic release and in some instances bring about an emotional healing process that we are unprepared for;

therefore it is important for us to remember to be kind to ourselves. Perhaps holding a rose quartz crystal may help or some may prefer a Bach flower remedy to be at hand.

Helpful tip: If not conversant with EFT then Nick Ortner's book 'The Tapping Solution' may help, or access his website www.thetapping. solution.com where it is possible to see a tapping routine in action.

14th August – A Wishing Box

Wishing boxes are adored by children and adults are also beginning to get in on the act, although we often call them 'angel' or 'blessing' boxes. A creative activity for today, whether on our own or with children or grandchildren, is to make a wishing box in which we place slips of paper with written requests for wishes and blessings for ourselves and others. Perhaps photographs of loved ones can also be placed in the box with a request written on the back. If a member of the family or a friend is pregnant, we can place their name in the box for them and the unborn baby to have a safe and healthy pregnancy and birth.

Our wishing boxes could be made from wood with decorative shells glued to the outside in a pattern; these basic blank boxes are found in many craft shops. We could also use a pretty box previously given to us, perhaps containing perfume, so that we upcycle this item. If we'd like to make it more of an angel box then we could glue a pretty collage of angel images. The Chinese consider the balance of one boy child and one girl child as a blessing, so their calligraphy for 'blessing' is these two outlines together. Perhaps this particular outline to decorate our blessing box may be favoured.

Helpful tip: If unable to locate the Chinese calligraphy outline for 'blessing' on the Internet, pay a visit to a local Chinese food store and they will probably be able to help.

16th August – Love Fun with Playing Cards

Let's have some light-hearted fun with 'love divination' (taking us back to our teenage years!) using a pack of playing cards by placing the Queen (or King) of Hearts, to represent ourselves, in front of us and shuffling the rest of the pack. When doing so, we think of what we desire from a loving relationship and then, one by one from the top, turn over the cards and place them into another pile.

If in the first 25 cards there appears the court card of the King (or Queen) of Hearts, the relationship will be lasting and settled. If in the first 25 cards the Jack of Hearts appears, then the relationship will be fun and exciting but possibly a short-term relationship. If both the court cards of Jack and King (or Queen) of Hearts appear, the relationship will be lasting *and* fun. But if the King (or Queen) of Clubs turns up before the other two cards, regardless of wherever it is in the pack, then the relationship will be challenging.

18th August – Roadside Assistance

As we travel our roads, we occasionally see a vehicle parked on the roadside verge with its bonnet up looking as if there is a mechanical problem. What do we do in these instances? Some of us are able to stop and offer assistance, even if all we do is 'phone for the appropriate roadside services; however, if we are a lone female, stopping to help may make us feel vulnerable and then we feel uncomfortable with ourselves for not being of service to someone – especially as we would appreciate outside help ourselves if faced with similar circumstances in the future.

There is something that can be done and that is to send a prayerful request for them to receive help, whether our prayer is to God, the angels or the universe, even if the roadside services are already in attendance. We generally do not know the situation for these people;

they may be attempting to visit a sick family member and timing is important, or they may be in financial trouble and be concerned about paying for repairs, or they may have a young baby on board who is fretting. The issues potentially facing them could be many, so we can do our little bit by praying for them to receive the help they need for their highest and greatest good. From today, let us try to remember this practice for when we next see a car needing roadside assistance.

20th August – Pressing Flowers

The fauna and flora of our land can be breathtaking, such as when we come across ancient bluebell dells or buttercup meadows, and we often try to capture these experiences with our cameras. Perhaps our garden has produced an especially wonderful display and we are proud of the blaze of colour and abundant life it has exhibited. The hobby of pressing flowers has waxed and waned in favour over the passing generations; however, today let's find some flowers to press and later use them to create a personalised greeting card.

Children can take part in this activity and enjoy the hands-on experience of choosing the flowers and then finding the heavy book with which to press them if we don't own a flower press. Take care not to pick wild flowers unlawfully if we don't have our own garden. Once dried, in around two weeks, they can be glued gently onto a card in a pattern shape or as part of an overall picture. The card can be personalised with a verse inside for a specific reason such as a birthday, anniversary, get well or for a new home. An example for a friend who is moving away to a new home could be:

"We wish you luck and all the best
as you start new life in another nest.
Here's a reminder as you go
of summer in a country hedgerow.

This card of flowers in collage
is to wish you joy and bon voyage."

22nd August – Prayer Flags

A common picture noticed when scenes of Tibet are shown is that of prayer flags as they flap in the winds in the high mountains. However, these flags are not limited to Tibet as many cultures throughout the world have used flags to represent various beliefs as we commune with the moving cycle of the Earth.

Today, we could try making our own prayer flags but with a little difference. Bunting has become popular in recent years and we could cut our prayer flags in triangular shapes to create the bunting effect. The colours of our flags will be those of our energy centres, our chakras: red for the base chakra, orange for the sacral chakra, yellow for the solar plexus, green for the heart, blue for the throat, indigo for the brow chakra and violet for the crown. We can make our prayer flags from spare material we may have at home or buy off-cuts from a local haberdashery shop. If we are not skilled in sewing, be assured that very little sewing is required. Start with a length of twine and wrap over it the edge of a 6" (15 cm) square of red material, and sew this in place on the string; then leave an inch space before sewing in place the orange square of material and so on in the order of the chakra colours.

We can make the length of our prayer flags longer by repeating the colour sequence, and we may like to hang them around the boundary of our garden. They are usually hung outdoors so that the winds can carry our prayers to the universe. While we sew the squares to the string, we can quietly pray or simply be in stillness thinking peaceful thoughts. Tibetan chanting could be played to help us focus on energising our chakras – and flags – with peaceful, healing and loving thoughts. When completed, we hang our prayer flags and request the wind to send our prayers for health to the universe.

Helpful tip: If without a garden, make a small set of prayer flags of about 2" (5 cm) square and drape them around a shrub we have in a tub outside our front door.

24th August – Hag Stones

In the popular 'Crocodile Dundee' film of 1986, he went up onto a high rock and used a bullroarer to create a sound calling his aboriginal friends to him. Bullroarers are also used as part of spiritual practices and ceremonies, when shamans work with the spirit realm. The sound bullroarers make when being spun like a lasso creates an energy vortex within the air that can be used to send our wishes to the universe (another form of cosmic ordering). We send our wish to the universe by being in a secluded spot in the country or perhaps on the seashore and send our bullroarer circling, all the while focusing on our desire.

However, bullroarers are rarely found in the UK and unless we wish to make our own we could try another option, using what are known as hag stones. These are stones that have a naturally eroded hole through them; the holes are usually caused by water continuously dripping onto the same spot for many years. The most common hag stones are of flint and these can be found on our beaches and riversides, although we might even find flint chippings in our gardens that have naturally eroded holes in them. We tie (securely!) a piece of twine or a long leather thong through the hole. Our hag stone can be decorated with acrylic paint if we'd like to make our own ceremonies more meaningful for us.

Today, try to find a hag stone and use this to send wishes while spinning lasso-style. We may prefer sending our wishes on a new moon to represent new beginnings, then use it again on a full moon to express our thanks.

26th August – The Hermit in Tarot

In the Tarot, the major arcana card of The Hermit is associated with Virgo and linked with soul-searching, discovering our own inner light and self-knowledge. So it suggests a time to retreat and reflect, to go inside ourselves and meditate. The Hermit may be considered a symbol of the spirit world, representing our ancestors, guides and angels who are there to help us along our pathway. To receive guidance on our journey, it is important for us to find moments when we feel at peace and are able to cultivate stillness in order to sense the other world – and our own intuitive answers – when pondering our options.

Summer is usually a busy time for us, being active with the long summer days. However, this can mean we become caught up with these many activities and become 'monkey brains' again, not listening to our intuition. It's great to have fun on happy, sunny days as this is surely a huge part of life – to live in joy – but occasionally it is preferable for us to withdraw for some me-time in stillness. Perhaps a long soak in the bath is the perfect solution in a busy family life! The Hermit suggests, when the sun is clearly showing signs of shorter days, the importance of finding occasional times to be in peace and to conduct a little internal reflection and soul-searching to help us on our way forward.

28th August – Hatha Yoga

There are several types of yoga, some of them very dynamic, and some yoga styles have grown in popularity as we see pictures of celebrities in magazines in various poses (known as *asanas*). However, those looking for a gentler introduction to yoga should perhaps choose Hatha. Whilst there are some dynamic poses in Hatha yoga, most positions are gained slowly with a smooth flow. It is a good practice from which to move on later should a more dynamic yoga style be of interest.

Hatha yoga enables us gradually to gain better suppleness in our bodies, no matter what age or what physical condition we are in. A good teacher will offer alternatives in a class: for example, while some are able to do an eagle pose and maintain balance with no support, a newcomer will be able to use a chair or wall for balance. Yoga helps us especially in learning to breathe properly by using different breathing techniques (such as the 'three-part breath' and 'mountain breathing'). We learn to focus on our bodies and on what each limb is doing, and thus adjust them as necessary, so mindfulness is a central part of this practice. Hatha yoga helps us to find a peaceful still-point and to be present with what we are doing, not thinking about other things such as planning our shopping list; this way our minds are able to find some peace. In terms of a physical boost to our bodies, it also encourages wellbeing for our internal organs and structures. For example, the shoulder stand (also known as 'the queen of stands') assists with thyroid health, whilst the simple 'cobbler' floor pose boosts circulation to and from our pelvic area.

Today, consider attending a Hatha yoga class nearby. Often at this time of the year we can find, say, ten-week courses in our local educational booklet; but many yoga teachers hold classes throughout the year in local halls and often advertise in health food outlets and libraries.

Helpful tip: Whilst there are many DVDs and books on yoga available, it is strongly recommended to attend a class with a dedicated instructor in the first instance. A good teacher will help us to move into and remain in the various poses as we should; otherwise we could be causing undue strain on our bodies without realising it.

30th August – One Day Lessons

There are many courses on offer during the educational year at our local colleges and at town and village halls. Whilst the majority of courses are full-time with qualifications to be gained at the end, there are many other opportunities for less academic learning opportunities. Examples are one-day lessons for activities such as basket weaving, felting, floristry, embroidery, beadwork, crochet, simple stained glass, cake decorating, eastern cuisine, art and pottery, and not forgetting preparations for Christmas such as making holly wreaths, table displays and tree decorations. For those wishing to learn more about social media, we can often find a workshop demonstrating how to set up and manage a blog or how to shop and sell safely online.

Let's investigate this today – there may be a Local Authority booklet, or information at the library – and find out if any of the one-day lessons are appealing. Perhaps this can be shared with friends so that we experience a fun day of learning in a supportive environment. This could become a regular event each autumn for us and, as we expand our learning in each area, so we can move on to other activities that further enhance our lives.

September

This is the month of the autumn equinox when once again balance is brought to mind. A new educational year begins and we may ourselves be learning at home by harvesting our fruits to make jams, chutneys and wines in preparation for the coming winter. Sloes from the blackthorn may be harvested from the hedgerows as sloe gin is a favourite tipple during the cold months. Our thoughts naturally flow, as did our ancestors', to ensuring that food is provided for the winter.

The moon this month is commonly known as the Harvest Moon and some festivals being celebrated are Rosh Hashanah, Ludi Romani, Mabon and the Festival of Fides.

2nd September – Vine Month (2nd – 30th September)

In the Vine Month, teamwork with others is the theme. Think of the harvest period when villagers and communities all pulled together in the past to bring in the harvest. Working in partnership with others is an opportunity for harmony to reign, and we might think about what we can do to achieve this in our tasks with others, whether with colleagues, family or friends. The Armed Forces are examples of getting on with people from all walks of life: living, eating, sleeping, working and learning together encourages teamwork, comradeship and esprit de corps. In civilian life this is not always so as the conditions and purposes are not the same. Yet teamwork has an important and vital role in our workplaces and if we find it's not present then maybe we could try to change things.

Instead of looking for and focusing upon the differences between people, which only leads to barriers and poor connections, let's look for common ground instead. A small chink in the barrier where commonality can be found could provide the foundation for great change. This can be tried in any scenario, be it family, friends or at work. The common ground can be worked upon gradually, fostering good relations so that it grows, possibly achieving excellent results. Once we see this energy flowing, we shall feel encouraged to do more in future.

Today is a time for some gentle reflection, then, about where teamwork was required (in whichever scenario) but was found lacking. Did certain characters clash, even though from our viewpoint there were similarities between them? Were we one of these characters? Perhaps that had been a difficult time but now we can alter our view of the situation and consider working better together to find common ground, for example in achieving deadlines for projects.

This reflective practice is not about blaming others or ourselves, rather about detaching from any emotive issues and instead seeing the wider picture. When such situations arise again in future we can be determined to work, and help others to do so, at focusing on the common ground and building comradeship.

4ᵗʰ September – Online Support Groups

With many of us signed up to various forms of social media – such as blogs and vlogs, Twitter, Snapchat and Pinterest to name a few – we know that the Internet does provide a huge amount of information that is worthwhile. A possible consideration today is to join an online support group, or 'vibe tribe', that offers learning opportunities. Many of these social networking groups offer regular newsletters, videos, and email contact; if we are discerning we can find a suitable one for our needs. There are specific support groups for those suffering from an illness, for example, or they can be for particular interests such as Tarot, crystals and angels. Some are available for anyone to access (commonly known as 'open access') whilst some have a limit on numbers.

If not for now, we can bear these online support groups in mind for the future when we might need further information and contact with others. If we know of a friend or a family member who has an illness or special interest, but feels rather isolated, we could search for an established support group for them.

6ᵗʰ September – Learning the Runes

For some, symbols are a fascinating draw, with their many outlines and hieroglyphs becoming a passion. One interesting divinatory practice using symbols, or ancient ideograms, is that of 'reading the runes'. Some psychics tune in with runes to assist their focus and many people chose a rune as a daily oracle to inform them about the potential of the day ahead.

The runic proto-Norse alphabet has many associations with mythology. Legend has it that the Norse god Odin hung from the world tree, the Yggdrasil, for nine days in order to gain knowledge of the runes.

Learning the runes for divination is a fascinating activity. We could even make our own rune set by choosing even-sized pebbles and painting the symbols on them, or by collecting common limpet shells from a beach and painting on the insides of the shells. There are twenty-four rune symbols, usually arranged in three groups of eight. Making our own set may have more resonance for us than purchasing from a shop; if we have a family member or friend who expresses an interest in runes then we could offer them a set we have made as a nice personal gift.

There are many books about how to work with runes – 'The Book of Runes' by Ralph Blum is good – but we can also check the Internet for information in the first instance.

It is possible to create what is known as a 'bind rune', a charm made by us for a specific reason, when we wish to use the energies of two or three runes amalgamated together. Perhaps we know of someone in the Armed Forces being posted overseas, facing a difficult and potentially dangerous situation, in which case we could blend the energy of *Algiz* for protection with that of *Inguz* for their health and wellbeing, especially for males. We would draw this bind rune on a card and ask them to carry it in their wallet, or we could paint it onto a clear quartz crystal keyring that they would use regularly while away. They may feel reassured by this talisman, and the energy of the quartz will help to amplify the bind rune.

Helpful tip: Another way of using a rune to enhance an aspect of our lives is to create a rune outline using crystals and keep it in place as a charm for a while until it has done its work. An example outline could be that of *Fehu*, for wealth, made from citrine crystals and placed in our wealth corner.

8th September – Recycle

Recycling helps Mother Earth so is very much a practice to adopt. Our rubbish goes to landfill and incinerators and wherever these sites are they have an impact on the environment with their emissions of greenhouse gases. Setting the intention to start recycling, or to extend what we already do, will help. Items to be recycled include plastic, paper, aluminium, metal, wood, glass, cardboard and small electrical goods, and collections are usually organised by our local councils. Many areas also offer specific sites where we ourselves can drop off tyres, textiles and larger things. These sites can also be salvage points such as for lead, from car batteries, and gold, from circuit boards. Let's not forget that biodegradable waste can be used for composting; even if we don't have our own garden, perhaps we know someone who would appreciate our composting efforts for theirs or for an allotment.

Of particular concern is the amount of plastic, especially polystyrene, being produced as it is either too expensive or too difficult to recycle. Examples of this are the single-use straws, cutlery and cups used in many cafés, the materials of which are difficult and expensive to separate. Some outlets are now offering a discount for those who bring their own re-usable mugs, in order to reduce the use of disposable cups.

From today, please let us do whatever we can to help Mother Earth by recycling as much as we possibly can and reducing our use of plastics.

10th September – A Rainbow of Fruit

It's good to eat a rainbow of foods, especially one of fruit in a home-made smoothie or juice! We are encouraged by health officials to eat a minimum of five fruit and veg each day; but many consider that seven is a better option, so why not make it a rainbow of seven fruit today, knowing that the colours are also associated with the spiritual chakras. Potential fruits are: strawberries, raspberries, cherries, cranberries, redcurrants, pomegranates, nectarines, peaches, oranges, mandarins, apricots, mangos, papayas, cantaloupe, water and honeydew melons, plums, lemons, bananas, pineapples, passion fruits, grapefruits, pears, apples, limes, kiwi fruits, grapes, pomelos, avocados, blueberries, blackberries, blackcurrants, plums and figs.

There's so much goodness here for our bodies and such wonderful concoctions of flavours we can create, not forgetting to add a few herbs and seeds into the blender to boost the benefit.

12ᵗʰ September – Guardian Angels

Many of us have been taught since childhood that we each have a guardian angel so it's natural that we would wish to see, hear, feel and sense them. Exponents of angel contact in recent years have been spiritual teachers such as Chrissie Astell, Kyle Grey and Lorna Byrne. Guided CDs have been produced offering meditations to help us to meet our guardian angels, whereby perhaps we can see them in our mind's eye, notice the colour of their garments or energies and even get a sense of what their names are.

Perhaps some of us have experienced signs of our guardian angel but have dismissed this, thinking that something we saw was a trick of our eyesight, the aroma of flowers we suddenly caught was not real or the comforting feeling of being gently embraced was our mind playing games as we drifted off to sleep after a difficult day.

When we ask our guardian angel to make themselves known to us, it is clearly important that we are open to the ways in which they are able to do this, such as those above. Instead of dismissing them, we should be grateful. We may ask our guardian angel to provide specific 'evidence', such as stating something unusual we wish to see on our journey to work; when this actually occurs we often still require further proof of their existence! It could be the case that we do see our guardian angel regularly but do not recognise them as such because they are not what we expect. Art since the Middle Ages has encouraged us to view angels with wings; however, perhaps our guardian angel appears wearing a long flowing cape – or may not appear in human form at all but as a coloured orb that hovers nearby when we specifically request their presence.

We should try opening our minds more to the ways that our guardian angel can make themselves known to us, be less dismissive of the tricks we believe our minds and eyesight are playing and instead monitor these occurrences and record them. We may find that these moments actually did arise when we were facing difficult scenarios and gradually we can then begin to understand the angels' presence.

14th September – Morning Routines

Many of us wake up to an alarm going off, with a groan as we come round, stumbling to reach for a dressing-gown and walking from room to room on remote control as we prepare ourselves for the day ahead. Unfortunately, this does not characterise a good start for the day!

So let's consider how we start our mornings. Do we awake already exhausted and dreading the day ahead? Do our bodies feel sluggish due to alcohol the previous night? Are we so disorganised that we are unable to find the right clothes? Do we not allow ourselves enough time, so that if problems arise we become late, adding hindrance and stress to our day?

We need to reflect on our morning routine and think about some changes we could create to enable our days to start with a good vibra-tion, even if this means altering other normal routines. Let's think outside the box about how we can achieve change and instead find joy in waking up with a high vibration to kick-start our morning each day.

We may find that simply saying "Good morning" each to Mother Earth, Father Sky, Brother Sun and Sister Moon (if still visible) has a beneficial effect, being the first words we utter when waking. What wonderful energies to acknowledge in the morning every day.

16th September – Pampering the Auric Body

Essential oils are used for many health and wellbeing reasons, whether as aromatherapy in diffusers or a few drops added to our massage oils or bath water. Lavender is a wonderful healer and is the only essential oil that can be used on our skin without dilution (if not allergic to it).

Some therapists like to dip their crystals into essential oils as they work with the auric fields, the energy fields surrounding our bodies, during a session. The aura protects us and, just as we like to maintain a healthy skin, we should also think about maintaining healthy auric fields. A simple way to do this is by using the essential oil of orange, placing one drop into our bathwater each week. This oil is good for the aura, helping to protect it and keep it healthy. Naturally, before starting this practice it is important to check for any allergic reaction; and if pregnant or with skin issues, do research beforehand to check that the use of this product is acceptable.

Helpful tip: If showering is preferred, it is still possible to pamper the aura with orange essential oil, using one drop in a small dish of water and occasionally adding a little of this liquid to a sponge as we wash.

18th September – Feng Shui

This suggestion is for improving our sleeping patterns by keeping the electrical items in our bedrooms to the bare minimum and ensuring that they are switched off at the mains when retiring. This includes our bedside lamps. Televisions, computers, mobile 'phones and radios in our bedrooms have an electromagnetic field energy that can disrupt our sleep. As good sleep is important for our general wellbeing, this is definitely something to be mindful of.

If our accommodation is limited and there is nowhere else to place these electrical items, then perhaps we could erect a screen around them at night or place a crystal such as sodalite nearby to soak up their EMF smog.

Helpful tip: Ensure that any crystal chosen for soaking up electro-magnetic smog is cleansed on a weekly basis.

20th September – Loving Hearts

Today, we could spend a little time thinking about what brings us joy, what we are grateful for, which activities encourage fun in our lives, whom we love and what we love. Firstly, we create a big heart shape on an A4 piece of paper – or A3 if we wish to make a big statement! We can draw or paint a heart shape ourselves, though it is also possible to print one from clip art examples on our computers.

As we trawl through our thoughts, each time one of the above comes to mind we write it within the heart shape. At first we may find this easy enough, such as writing the names of our family and friends as well as our pets, being grateful for our homes, jobs and cars, and for the joy gained from our hobbies, walking the countryside or relaxing in the garden.

Then after a while the things to write may dry up and this is where we can think creatively. We can think of our favourite food, maybe even chocolate, so this can be written in the heart; perhaps our favourite fragrances can be added as usually these uplift us. Let's not forget being grateful for clean drinking water from our taps and for simply flicking a switch for heating and lighting. Perhaps a love of sport can be included to reflect our interests.

Once we have completed our hearts we can place them on our fridges or noticeboards as a gentle reminder to express gratitude for what we love and enjoy in our lives.

22nd September – Bibliomancy

Another divinatory tool we can try today is known as bibliomancy, and all that is required is a book. When we shuffle our oracle cards or Tarot decks, and intend to pull one card to consider for the day or to help us find an answer to a question, we probably have a 'go to' set of cards that we prefer to use. The same divinatory practice can be done with bibliomancy, using a favourite book. The Bible was used in times past for this, but nowadays a thesaurus could be used, or a dictionary, or even a favourite novel.

It's easy to try: all we do is hold the book and close our eyes, considering the question we wish to ask. Then, still with eyes closed we open the book at a random page and allow the forefinger of our non-dominant hand to stop at any point on the open spread of the two pages. We then open our eyes and read the entry, sentence or phrase where the finger has stopped. If the sentence is of help to us, we only need to do this once. If the sentence is not entirely helpful we could have another go to aid our understanding further. It is possible to do this a third time so that the overall picture of three sentences expands the meaning and helps us formulate a possible way forward. This is similar to drawing three oracle cards, when sometimes one just does not cover what we are looking for.

Helpful tip: If we have a book on crystals, we could try bibliomancy with this as it could be that the crystal's energy is required for us too.

24th September – Opal, the Libra Birthstone

The precious gem of 'quality opal' is very beautiful with its many shimmering colours; however, a member of this family that is quite inexpensive as a tumble stone is fire opal. Fire opal can aid our meditation or prayer practices and would be a good crystal to hold at these times. It assists in intensifying our experiences somewhat and so when meditating or in meditative prayer any blissful or peaceful emotions will be felt more deeply. Let's research fire opal today and allow it to provide insightful reflections as we instigate our changes and evaluate our journey's progress.

26th September – Rosh Hashanah, the Jewish New Year

Around this time is Rosh Hashanah, a Jewish ritual ten days before Yom Kippur (the Day of Atonement), when thoughts are focused on putting things right with others. We can all use this time as a reminder for us to learn that it is far better to understand the possible consequences of our actions, and not allow something to occur in the first instance, than dealing with the subsequent fallout. This is along the lines of 'prevention being better than the cure' so that we have little, if anything, to put right.

Maybe we can consider how often we make forceful decisions with family and friends and then, to save face, we follow through with these decisions despite wishing we had never made them in the first instance – they really were not in anyone's best interest, so we can be left with bitter memories. Let us reflect upon rash decisions or ultimata we may have made in the past, which led us on a path we now wish we had never entertained. Perhaps we listened to the ego rather than to the heart. These situations may be linked with our employment, with our family or a group we belong to. We need to try and understand the ego's part in making decisions and be prepared to learn from these experiential opportunities, listening and paying more attention to our hearts when making decisions.

This reflective time may bring up some upsetting emotions as when we express ourselves too forcefully this can return to haunt us in later years, with dark energy buried deep in our psyche for a long time. Magnesite is a helpful stone to hold in these instances as it can help to calm our emotions; it also has a link with egotism, teaching us to listen actively rather than always needing to be in the driving seat. Another good crystal is the commonly available chrysoprase, sold as a tumble stone, which aids our reflective practices where ego has played a part. Throughout all of this it would also be helpful to be near some rose quartz for its loving and compassionate energies.

We are unable to change what we did or said in the past, but we can change the outcome for ourselves by allowing peace for the body, mind and spirit concerning past upsets. This could be achieved with a prayer to Source expressing our truth of the matter and asking for help to find a way forward at this time of Rosh Hashanah.

Helpful tip: Bach flower remedies may be helpful and also tapping, if our emotions start to overwhelm us.

28th September – Conker Luck

Many believe that horse chestnut conkers are lucky, so for a simple lucky charm today let's collect some and string them together to hang up in our homes. As we string each conker, we make a wish that it brings good things our way such as excellent health, strength, financial security, love, new friendships, a new job or exam success. We keep the conker lucky charm in place until Christmas or Yule and then bury it in the ground with our thanks.

Helpful tip: To add more potency, we could draw a rune symbol (see 6th September) on each conker to reflect our particular wish for luck.

30th September – Workplace Carbon Footprint

We have our own responsibilities of carbon footprint in terms of how we live at home and in our everyday activities, but what about our workplaces? There is often much wastage in our workplaces so, if we are able to get involved in ensuring these organisations pay attention to this important matter, then we can help this beautiful Earth. A good many workplaces already have recycling facilities, yet there are many more options available. The larger organisations may even have their own committees for this issue and maybe we could take an active part by becoming a member. Perhaps we could ask others involved in reducing carbon footprint to visit our workplaces, give a talk and make recommendations specific to our site. Let us be open to what is possible.

We can play our part too every day, no matter how small. If a light is on when not required, then we can switch it off. We can turn off electrical machinery at the socket when leaving the workplace for the day instead of using the standby facility. We can advocate paperless working wherever and whenever possible.

It is important for us to consider our future generations. The great Mahatma Ghandi said, "Live simply so that others may simply live." This should be a rallying call for us to remember every day.

October

We are well into autumn now with our footwear disappearing beneath the fallen leaves as we traverse through the countryside, parks and tree-lined pavements. It's definitely a chilly time, with winter hats coming out of the closet again.

This month is the Frost Moon and celebratory events are Gandhi Jayanti, Samhain (Hallowe'en) and Meditrinalia.

OCTOBER

2ⁿᵈ October – A Spiritual Store Cupboard

Keeping our spiritual tools, supplies and books in one place rather than being scattered around the home offers respect for their energetic vibrations as well as helping us to be organised. As we access our spiritual store cupboard we are then aware that these tools have been kept in an atmosphere of spiritual love and compassion ready for use.

Examples of items to be held here are incense sticks, oracle cards, Tarot cards, runes, spell books, altar cloths, crystals, candles, wands, and not forgetting items for charm work, say, magical salt, dried herbs, shells, feathers, various coloured ribbons and any hedgerow harvest such as dried bramble barbs. This special cupboard could be a specific trunk, perhaps a blanket box or ottoman which would not look out of place in a bedroom. It may be suitable for a wall cupboard in the kitchen to be set aside, or a certain section of a wardrobe could store our items.

Today we could spend a little time bringing all of our spiritual tools together and consider where they could be stored in one place so that we create our spiritual store cupboard.

Helpful tip: Once we have created our store, we can charge it with a blessing of intent in whichever way we wish, perhaps with an incense stick; or if we have a rose quartz crystal in a heart shape we could place this in the centre so that its compassionate energies reminds us always to work with love.

4ᵗʰ October – World Animal Day

Mahatma Gandhi said, "The greatness of a nation and its moral progress can be judged by the way its animals are treated." Today is World Animal Day and also the feast day of St Francis of Assisi, the patron saint of all animals. Let us visit, or plan a visit to, an animal

147

rescue centre and offer our love and companionship to the animals. Whichever sanctuary or rescue centre visited, these animals deserve to be treated with love and compassion.

At these centres, the animals are in a place where they are cared for and looked after properly, receiving the love, care and attention they need until a new home can be found. We could spend some time at the rescue centre giving our time and offering love and fuss to the rescued animals. It is important to note that not all animals have been 'a cruelty case' as a great many are there due to purely social restrictions such as an elderly person entering a care home or perhaps a relationship has broken down and the new accommodation does not allow for pets. These scenarios can be emotionally traumatising for the pets and some can develop separation anxiety, so it would be a wonderful gesture to visit a centre and offer our attention to them.

We may find that we enjoy the experience and decide to volunteer a little of our time each week to the centre. Perhaps we could be a dog walker at the weekend, or maybe we prefer to sit with the cats and kittens playing with them, helping to enrich their lives at a difficult time of adjustment for them.

Helpful tip: Some of us may not wish to visit a cat or dog rescue centre as we fear a very cute kitten or puppy may weaken any resolve we may have regarding adopting one of them! However, if we can change our perspective to that of knowing the animal has already been rescued and is in a safe place, we therefore do not have to rescue it. The cat or dog is waiting for a new home, which is not necessarily ours. Another option would be to visit another centre such as a seal or wild bird sanctuary where we are unable to bring one home with us and do not experience a sense of guilt when leaving.

6th October – Hibernation Study

The time of year will soon be arriving when Mother Earth hibernates. It is also a time for humans to follow this natural cycle and use the ensuing dark evenings to reflect on the past year and prepare for the spring when it will be time to flourish once again. In nature, although most of the plants and trees have died back and shed their foliage, underground they are waiting to push outwards once again when the natural cycle is ready. Why not take this time ourselves today to reflect and plan a course of study in order to aid our own growth, so that we too can burgeon forth in the spring?

A course of study can be anything such as researching over a period of time on the Internet a particular subject we wish to learn about; if the subject matter is something we've been promising ourselves to do for a long time then why not set the intention today? Perhaps attending a class with others may be preferred, or we would like to set ourselves a specific reading project at home to understand its foundations, such as 'A Course in Miracles'.

These hibernation months are a good time for this sort of activity when it fits in with the lifestyle of being indoors during the dark evenings of autumn and winter.

8th October – Coaching

Coaching is a very useful approach in life for everyone to consider. It enables us to think about the many aspects of a situation and encourages us to question ourselves, to enable self-growth whether personally or professionally. It is also of help when having difficult conversations with our children or work colleagues and helps us to stop 'rescuing' others and instead guide them to find their way forward. Coaching is not linked to one particular subject matter or endeavour but encompasses the many aspirations of humans as we evolve. It can help us to reach our potential – even if we are only starting on our journey and not fully aware of where it might lead us. Our potential grows with us as we gain experience. It enables us to understand some of our fears and can guide us to work through challenges. The process can help to enlighten us by recognising previous patterns of behaviour and in doing so assist us in redefining our old inhibited responses to bring about change. Our journeys in life rarely, if ever, follow a straight pathway and as we change directions (sometimes known as 'zig-zagging' in coaching) to cater for our ongoing evolution, navigating our way forward from a coaching perspective can be key to successful achievements.

There are many questions we can ask ourselves to enable us to move forward, such as: What did I learn from this process? What is in the way that stops me moving forward? How did I solve a similar problem before and would it work in this instance? What is the next step taking me closer to my goal? What action would make the biggest difference? What options are available to resolve this? Is this a hindrance or part of the solution? What elements are outside of my control? What needs to happen for an outcome? If I don't take any action, what will happen? Is this the best outcome or is there something even better? This type of self-searching question move us from great to greater and on to greatest.

Then, of course, there is also what is known as 'magic wand thinking' whereby we allow our minds to have the freedom to run riot for a while and to imagine all sorts of scenarios and solutions; some may be considered pie-in-the-sky and occasionally quite comical, but out of this brainstorming creativity can pop an answer or a step forward. We can ask ourselves questions starting off with: If I had a magic wand and there were no limitations... How would I solve this problem? What is my ideal solution? If I removed *(something)* from the equation, what outcome would that achieve? If I had control over *(something)* how would this affect the situation? What would I turn around in this scenario? What would I do differently if I had the chance to start this again? What new skill could I develop to leap forward?

Today, let's research coaching and try adopting some of its techniques for moving forward in our lives in whichever way we feel is required. Coaching has become very popular and we may find that as we adopt some of its practices and feel comfortable with the processes, our goals and solutions become more focused and inspired. We may realise that we gradually cease any self-sabotage or procrastinating patterns and challenge our fear-based assumptions.

Another important change may be that we stop rescuing other people and instead use coaching questions to enable them to move forward. In doing so we shall have more free time for ourselves as we have not become involved in sorting out their problems.

10th October – A Guided Meditation

Often, at home after a busy day, many people are happy to relax and play a guided meditation, on a CD or `phone app, as it brings about a different sense of relaxation. This is a similar feeling to when, say, we have been invited to friends for Sunday lunch: we enjoy the food that somebody else has cooked and we've relinquished the reins of planning, prepping and cooking it all. A guided meditation CD provides a similar relaxation of organisation; we can simply 'go with the flow'.

It's important to be discerning in respect of the meditations to use, and mindful that they fulfil our requirements. When we have some that suit us perfectly it feels like 'wearing an old pair of comfortable slippers' and we are soon ready for a period of peacefulness. We may even find ourselves relishing the prospect of listening to these guiding words on arriving home after a stressful day at work.

There are hundreds of guided meditation CDs and apps available now and range from angels to Buddhist mantras, with many being orated by well-known people. Some are also produced to help us with our learning such as 'The Fool's Journey' by Tiffany Crosara, which is a guided meditation helping us to understand the archetypes of the Tarot's Major Arcana cards and useful for those wishing to learn Tarot.

Look into this option today. If we already have one or two, then perhaps try a little expansion by considering a guided meditation outside our usual range.

Helpful tip: Most of us have access to recording facilities, from anti-quated cassette tape machines to our mobile 'phones, and these could be used to create our own meditations. Sometimes we experience inspired moments in our lives, perhaps a seaside vista or a beautiful country walk, and wish to create meditations from these to repro-duce the peacefulness we felt. These are wonderful opportunities to capture and record our own guided meditations.

12th October – Palmistry

'Reading' our bodies has been around for a long time and includes body language and iridology as well as the commonly known but ancient practice of palm reading. Palm readers are found in many countries and cultures. Courses of study can be undertaken with a diploma to be gained or we can visit an intuitive or a medium who uses palmistry as a tool for their readings.

When palm readers look at and hold our hands, they make many observations such as their dryness, colour and shape as well as the lines. They also look at the dorsal side of our hands and not just our palms. Whilst our fingerprints do not change, other lines on our hands do and because of this many people wish to have a reading on an annual basis.

Today, let's look into palmistry and perhaps find a palm reader in the local area for a chat and maybe book a session with them. It is important to be discerning about whom we see – it may be prefera-ble to visit someone who is highly recommended by word of mouth but has a waiting list, indicating their excellent reputation and being worth waiting for.

14th October – The Cycles of Life

We live our lives in cycles: we are born, grow into childhood and then teenage years, mature into adulthood, age into our crone years and then transition to spirit. The cycle of Earth is similar. Imbolc marks the start of the Earth stirring into life. The spring equinox sees growth sprouting, followed by Beltane in May when Mother Earth has quickened and she bursts forth in much profusion. At the summer solstice, or Litha, there are signs of grain and fruits forming and by Lammas we start our first harvests. Mabon at the autumn equinox sees further harvests and by Samhain this is the final harvest of nuts. Then the Earth dons its hibernating mantle for sleep by the time of the winter solstice, Yule.

Our ancestors worked with this cycle of Mother Earth, observing her natural death and rebirth, and honoured the food freely given by her to sustain life. The sun and moon played a part in understanding these cycles, so also the wildlife such as when bears hibernated, certain fish appeared in rivers to spawn and when the wild horses bore foals. They would have looked to the shamans or spiritual leaders of their clan to understand these cycles and know when the ceremonies were to be held in celebration of the passing seasons.

When the human population grew and spread out across the land, the Christian Church's ceremonies and saints' days became the focal point in European countries for guidance on when to work the land to be in tune with her cycles of life. Examples of these are St Barnabas Day on 11th June, when sheep shearing and hay making would be started; St Swithin's day on 15th July saw mutton slaughtered; on St Lawrence's Day, the 10th August, grain threshing started; winter grain was sown on St Luke's Day, 18th October; St Jude's Day on 28th

October indicated the end of fine weather; on All Souls' Day, the 2nd November, acorns were harvested to fatten pigs in preparation for the feasting in December.

In recent years we have begun creating extra growing seasons by the use of polytunnels, greenhouses and hydroponics, so much food is grown outside of Mother Earth's cycle. We have also taken to using chemical methods to protect our crops and extended this to genetically modified foods. However, there are still some who have returned to the old ways of growing crops and who follow the moon cycles for knowing when to sow, plant and harvest.

Today, we could research the following of moon cycles and also the Middle Ages practices of growing and harvesting food when the Christian calendar of saints and other celebrations had a bearing (known as the Liturgy calendar). Perhaps we may see some similarities between the two and it may be that for our own gardens we decide to try planting and harvesting by the moon.

16th October – Feng Shui

If we are looking for a loving relationship, or if already in one and wish for love to continue to flourish, then we could place a vase of two silk red roses in the far right corner of our bedroom. This particular corner is located from the point of view of entering the room. It is important to clean the silk roses regularly to keep them free of dust!

18th October – Practise Seeing Auras

As mentioned previously, our bodies have an energy field known as the auric field, or aura, and some people are able to see this quite naturally. Not only are they able to see the auras of humans but also those of animals, plants and crystals. Occasionally, we may have inadvertently seen our own aura simply by daydreaming and allowing our eyes to soften and lose focus as we sip a drink, noticing a colour extending away from our hands.

A common colour seen in the auras of healers is turquoise, and violet is often seen in the auras of mediums. Any area of illness or dis-ease in our bodies can also be recognised by those who observe our auras; for example, if we have a broken bone there will be another type of fracture seen in our auric field, such as a grey area where the broken bone is situated. This is a fascinating subject to read about and Anne Jirsch's book 'Instant Intuition' is informative, as is 'Auras: what they are and how to read them' by Joseph Ostrom.

We could try seeing our aura this evening by having on a dim light and looking at a mirror, full-length if possible. Then we un-focus our eyes for a few minutes. Initially, we may only see perhaps a slight off-white colour as an outline of our body shape; however, it is worth practising as eventually we could discern more and more of our aura.

Helpful tip: The incredibly adept traffic policemen of India's cities often use the unfocused eyes of yoga's 'eagle pose' to help them guide the traffic, so perhaps regularly practising the eagle pose before attempting to see the aura may be a good idea.

20th October – Cloud Divination

Cloud divination is also known as nephelomancy, aeromancy or cloud scrying. From today, let's start paying more attention to cloud formations, observing them and seeing what outlines they make. We can check if they make a formation that represents something strongly resonating with us, such as two clouds seeming to form a handshake by two people. This could urge us to reflect about ways of achieving good relationships, which could be rather pertinent for us at the time. Cloud divination can be tried regularly for ten minutes every day or maybe we would prefer to scan the clouds quickly each time we look up to the sky. What we could try is to ask a question in the morning and then during the course of the day occasionally check the clouds to see if there are any formations that seem to provide an answer.

Occasionally, spectacular cloud outlines can be formed and sometimes photographs of formations appear in the newspapers due to them looking like angels, for example. Perhaps we should always ensure that we have our mobile `phones or cameras with us to capture an impressive cloud formation, especially as they change rapidly on windy days.

Helpful tip: Not only is the shape of the cloud used to help us but also their type, such as cumulus or stratus. Some of these specific clouds have cautionary interpretations whilst others offer reassurance and perhaps good fortune, so researching these clouds with their specific divinatory meanings may be of interest.

22nd October – Build a Cairn

Today, we could try setting aside or planning some time to collect some flat stones and build a cairn with them. In conducting this activity we may find that our breathing and heart rate slow, we slip into mindfulness and become almost meditative in our thoughts as this quiet time allows space for peaceful contemplation. The ancients built cairns for varying reasons, such as marking the site of a grave in the Bronze Age, whilst other cultures used them as shrines or simply as road markers for travellers.

We may also wish to make the building of cairns a fun activity with family and friends on a beach picnic or by a stony riverside, and have a light-hearted competition for who can build the highest cairn in a set period of time. In many wellbeing and Zen pictures, we often see rounded stones balanced one on top of another to indicate a calming perspective, and perhaps a few of the best flat and rounded stones can be taken home and placed as a small cairn on a shelf or in the garden to remind us of the importance of being balanced. If we have a small figure of Buddha, we could paint some of these rounded stones in a gold colour and balance them on each side of Buddha in our meditation area.

24th October – United Nations Day

The United Nations Charter came into being on 24th October, 1945. The UN encourages respect for human rights and freedom for all and deem these as fundamental for all peoples throughout the world, encouraging friendly relations so that international co-operation can be achieved. Today, let's take this ethos of thinking from the international stage into our own communities.

We could consider how we can help to develop friendly relations with our neighbours. Is there the possibility of organising an event where the whole community can gather and co-operate with one another, thus encouraging increased harmony? Has there been an occasion where perhaps a lack of respect in the past does not sit well with us and now there is an opportunity to put this behind us and change the outcome of this particular story?

Like small acorns growing into big oak trees, small efforts on our part to engender improved relations with the immediate world around us could be the start of a new phase of community harmony. With Samhain just around the corner, this could be an opportunity for organising something for the children in the area too, so that they can enjoy this celebration in a safe and happy way as neighbours gather together; one possibility is to arrange a party for the children with ghoulish fancy dress and old-fashioned games such bobbing apples.

26th October – Tourmaline

There are several tourmalines: black, pink, red, green, blue, golden, brown, watermelon, clear (known as achroite) and multi-coloured (known as elbaite). Watermelon tourmaline is an incredibly beautiful crystal and, depending upon the way the crystal is cut, shows wonderful patterns of pink and green. These two colours are connected to the heart chakra and this crystal is known for helping to heal emotional conflict which, when out of balance, can block our heart centres.

Watermelon tourmaline is also believed to help us with our intentions so, if we run out of steam or our motivation is flagging a little during our journey and we require some back-up, then watermelon tourmaline is a good choice. Another quality it has is that of helping us to find our quiet point, our stillness and calming centre in preparation for meditation. Today, we could research watermelon tourmaline and hopefully obtain a piece we are attracted to and enjoy its energies and beauty.

28th October – The Akashic Records

Some spiritual teachers refer to the Akashic Records as being 'the Book of Life' and held in the spiritual Great Halls of Learning. Courses for learning about the Akashic Records are becoming more popular; some clairvoyants and mediums will access the Akashic Records when we have a reading with them to assist us in moving forward in life.

Guided CDs have been produced to help us 'visit' the Akashic Records in our meditations at home – we may be guided to see vast halls or cathedrals made of crystal and lined with books. Some may visit the Akashic Records while undergoing a past life regression, going into a state known as 'between lives' where they find themselves sitting with a huge book filled with writing, sigils and images.

Although accessing the book and seeing outlines and images, we usually remain entirely unclear what these outlines may mean, as though they were an alien language!

Today, we could research the Akashic Records and see if this is something we would like to understand further.

30th October – Purchase Local Foods

Purchasing local foods wherever and whenever possible helps our local community as well as the planet, as in doing so we cut out air and road miles. If the local food is organic, then so much the better. Perhaps from today we could consider this option and look into what is possible for us to do. In our research we may come across a local collective of organic produce or find a pick-your-own facility, an activity to be shared with our children in the fresh air and used for education about where our food come from. Farmers' markets have become very popular and offer us another outlet for food on our doorstep, as well as the longstanding Women's Institute markets and country markets in local halls. Many local independent butcher shops often advertise the farm where their meat is sourced and this also appeals to shoppers wishing to buy local food.

This change in food source may be all the impulse we need to kick-start an intention to eat more healthily. It is worth understanding that as soon as we harvest any fruit and vegetable crop, its energetic vibration, previously provided by the plant as a whole, starts to wane and therefore the sooner we are able to consume the food the more of its natural energy we are able to take into our bodies. This natural energy is often known as 'the Mother', suggesting that it is the essence of the plant and its beneficial nutrients. Food nourishes, protects, strengthens and heals us, and when we do eat our meals we can also honour the food by chewing slowly and paying attention to the senses they create with their wonderful flavours.

Helpful tip: The practice of blessing and expressing grateful thanks to our garden herbs and plants is part of the spiritual way, so if we're at a pick-your-own facility it would be respectful for these plants also to be similarly blessed and thanked.

November

We are now moving from autumn into winter, the heating is on and we're getting the warmer clothes out of storage. The time for hibernation is almost upon us, a time of healthy introspection and planning new goals.

It's the Birch Moon this month and we celebrate Martinmas, All Saints' Day, All Souls' Day, the Feast of St Cecelia, Dia de las Muertos (Day of the Dead), Mischief Night, the Feast of Woden, Pomona, the Makahiki Festival and the Festival of the Lunantishees.

2nd November – Wallpaper Gift Boxes

Making small gift boxes from end rolls of wallpaper that are no longer needed is a pleasant and very quick activity that can quite easily be done while watching the television during the evenings. By the end of the evening, it is possible to have created several gift boxes ready to use for Christmas, birthdays or anniversaries, or perhaps as pretty boxes for wedding favours if a big event is looming.

The template used to guide us could be, for example, a cardboard box of tea bags commonly found in a supermarket. Choose whichever size appeals, or a variety of sizes. We carefully prise the box apart and lay it flat on the back of the wallpaper, then draw around the outline in pencil before cutting out with scissors. The next step is to create folds in the wallpaper in the same places as our template. Once the wallpaper is clearly folded we can then start building it into the box shape with glue or double-sided tape.

An alternative to using patterned wallpaper – we might prefer a blank canvas instead to create patterns with stars, circles or other sticky pictures – is to purchase a roll of plain white wallpaper for a small outlay. (But note that Anaglypta or flock types will not stick together.)

Helpful tip: Double-sided tape is preferable to glue as it sticks immediately. Pastel pinks, blues and greys in a striped wallpaper make perfect wedding favour boxes.

4th November – Mischief Night

Traditionally, this was a night when youngsters played tricks on neighbours, friends and family. Today though, let's bring in the grown-ups too and have some fun. We could organise a get-together with family and friends and play card or board games, or book up for a mystical event such as a tea-leaf reader, a Tarot reader or even a magic show. We could watch a comedy programme or film, play charades or do something to encourage much laughter. Whatever we choose to do, this is a day for enjoyment. Have fun and plenty of laughter and also add in one or two tricks to keep in tune with the night of mischief.

6th November – The Greek Goddess Hestia

This ancient Greek goddess was ruler of the hearth, home, domesticity and the family. In early November we are well and truly into autumn with the cold winter months very soon to be upon us and we can begin to relish the thought of being cocooned in our warm and cosy homes during this cold season.

Today, light a candle and spend a little quiet time reflecting with gratitude for our own domestic situations: our homes as shelter, our food as nourishment and our heating for warmth and comfort. The next step is to request help in prayer for those who are without a home and living on the streets. We can pray for their safety, that they receive appropriate healthcare, have warm clothing, find overnight shelter and receive enough food from the charity kitchens found in every town and city.

Finally, we can make a resolution to help the homeless in whatever way we can, such as by donating food, warm coats and perhaps blankets to the philanthropic organisations that help them.

8th November – Aromatherapy

There are so many wonderful aromas and such lovely ways to use them in aromatherapy. They are soothing, calming, uplifting, revitalising and healing. As Professor Snape said in 'Harry Potter and the Philosopher's Stone', magical herbal potions "ensnare the senses", so too does aromatherapy with its use of aromatic qualities.

There are many books available that offer guidance for home use but it is important to remember that they are not always a substitute for seeking a qualified aromatherapist. A doctor should also be consulted, especially in pregnancy and for some diagnosed illnesses, before attempting to use essential oils ourselves. Aromatherapy has become so popular that many High Street chemists and health shops now sell essential oils. The practice has been around for centuries, being used by the ancient Egyptians and Romans. The herbalist, Nicholas Culpeper, used the essential oils of specific herbs in his treatment regimes in the 1600s.

Simply dabbing a drop of lavender essential oil to our pulse points after a stressful day can be therapeutic in providing a sense of relaxation. Vapourisation of essential oils can be a good air freshener and cleanser of impurities; tea tree could be considered, as it has qualities of disinfecting the air if someone with a cold has visited, or indeed if we ourselves are suffering a cold. Using certain oils in a bath is an easy option and of course using them just for their aroma is a wonderful way of producing our own signature perfume.

Today, let's investigate aromatherapy for ourselves, our family and even our pets. We may find that these oils can make a significant and natural difference to our everyday lives.

Helpful tip: A well-known book to help us understand aromatherapy and its uses is 'The Fragrant Pharmacy' by Valerie Ann Worwood. However, if we wish to consider aromatherapy as an aid for our spiritual journey, we could consider 'The Fragrant Heavens' by the same author.

10th November – A Poem for Peace

As various countries in the world continue to experience war, conflict or terrorism, let us today turn our minds to peace again. The 11th November is Armistice Day, when peace was declared ending the

First World War, and we could prepare a poem in preparation for 11 a.m. tomorrow. Our poem would be based on expressing what peace means in our hearts. It doesn't have to be shared with anyone and can be ceremoniously burned or cast into the sea after reading it out tomorrow if we wish.

We can link this poem for peace to a specific country from the past or present, to our own experiences or to those of family or friends. Perhaps current events in the news may provide the impetus to write a poem of peace with them in mind. We can write our poem about individuals or all peoples of a nation. It is not necessary for the poem to rhyme, just write what peace means and feels like in our hearts.

If we wish to hold a small, special ceremony for peace, we could light a white candle and, before reading the poem, dedicate it to all those who have suffered in wars and conflicts and for those who continue to suffer. Animals can also be included as many horses and dogs suffered hugely by their service, as well as livestock caught in the middle of battles. Having read our poem out, we can burn it in the candle flame and request Archangel Sandalphon to carry our thoughts to the Source.

Helpful tip: *Haiku* (pronounced hi-queue) poetry may be appealing for us to try in this instance. It is a Japanese style in which only three lines make up each verse. Each line is very short using just a few words with the first line being five syllables, seven syllables for the second line and back to five syllables for the third line. Our wording does not have to rhyme and this style helps us to write from our hearts with minimal but very meaningful words, expressing succinctly what we feel.

12th November – Healing Foods

Our foods contain many compounds that aid our general health and today we could research this aspect more deeply. We may come across many illuminating examples. For example, any inflammatory condition is helped by ginger, bulgar wheat or pineapple; indeed, if it is necessary to take tablets, then taking them with pineapple juice helps the tablets to travel through our bodies to do their work quickly due a substance contained within the juice. Cherries are good for gout conditions and can keep away gouty conditions if regularly consumed. If giving up smoking, then liquorice and macadamia nuts eaten together can help to alleviate the withdrawal effects. The wonderful aromatic herb of spearmint helps to balance the hormones in our bodies.

It is becoming more popular now to investigate healing foods for any health issues encountered. This is often done to complement conventional treatments but also considered as routine dietary intake for preventative measures and maintaining optimum general good health. Let us open another world of health options today for ourselves and our families with healing foods.

Helpful tip: Neal's Yard Remedies of Covent Garden has produced a book entitled 'Healing Foods: eat your way to a healthier life', which is an excellent resource.

14th November – An Advent Calendar

Today there's a creative activity we may wish to try and prepare, offering uplifting and encouraging words in an advent calendar for the month of December for our family or our work colleagues. This year is gradually drawing to a close and perhaps for many there have been events that caused a stumble on the way; whilst we can acknowledge that stormy seas are our teachers, it is good to know that the New Year looming will encourage us in a new start. Our new start may be a change in our way of thinking or behaving, a new job, a new home or a new family. Our human lives form one big story, sometimes challenging and sometimes easy, but in whatever phase we find ourselves it is always good to read or hear uplifting words of encouragement. So let us offer these words of encouragement by creating our own special advent calendar.

Cut off an A3 size of good quality Christmas wrapping paper that has a pleasant pattern, or perhaps plain gold may be more appealing. If possible, the calendar can be strengthened by gluing the paper onto card. Next, we glue small envelopes to the patterned side of the paper in a random fashion, with the sealing edge of the envelope facing outwards. Then we number the envelopes 1 to 25 and inside each one we pop a wrapped sweet and an uplifting phrase before sealing the envelope. This is now ready for our family or to take in to work for 1st December.

Uplifting phrases or words of encouragement can be these: I move forward in my life with ease and joy; I live life and I love life; I embrace my journey with love and compassion for myself; I am adaptable, capable and resilient; opportunities are all around me; I allow my future to unfold; I greet each day with joy.

If we have a specific person in mind for our calendar, then try to make the phrases appropriate for them.

Helpful tip: For further inspiration about uplifting phrases to add to the advent calendar, then www.actionforhappiness.org may be a useful website to find resonating phrases. Louise Hay's classic book 'You Can Heal Your Life' is also a good port of call.

16th November – Feng Shui

Clearing clutter from our homes is an important part of Feng Shui. One very important area to consider is the entrance to our home, including the porch or hallway where we enter, the steps outside leading to the front door, the pathway and our front gate. These areas welcome auspicious abundance into our homes and in order for this to be activated it is vital for them to be clean and clear of excessive furniture and ornaments, with any coats preferably in a cupboard along with any footwear. Ensure that steps outside are kept clear, although red geraniums either side of the door are helpful. The same applies for the pathways by not blocking them with garden ornaments as the path is meant to allow energy to flow easily towards our front door. If we have a gate then it needs to open fully without any items blocking it.

Helpful tip: Whilst minimalism in our homes can look rather clinical, it is something to consider when decluttering our entrances.

18th November – What Brings on our Beaming Smiles?

When we walk along our pavements and notice the people nearby, we generally find very few of them smiling and instead see that many seem weighed down by concern and stress. A simple thing to do today is to reflect on how much we smile, or how little. If we realise that we could do with smiling more often, an option would be simply to do more of whatever does bring on our beaming smile. Do we like being around cats? Do we like watching the antics of dogs playing on a beach? Do we enjoy being with our friends for a lazy afternoon tea? Does immersing ourselves in a good book bring about a feel-good factor that leads to smiling more often? Can memories of past events with our children bring a smile to our face? There are so many choices to consider that do not involve spending money to achieve this state.

Even if there is nothing in particular to smile about, perhaps we could try smiling anyway! This is a little similar to laughter in that we 'fake it until we make it', a deliberate habit that eventually becomes natural. When at work, try gently smiling as we converse on the telephone or in person to our work colleagues – this also softens the voice. We could smile at our fellow customers on the supermarket checkout and at the cashier as we arrive for our turn. Let's try smiling more often from today and brighten the world as well as ourselves.

20ᵗʰ November – Universal Children's Day

Universal Children's Day was established in 1954 and although we may not be aware of it we will certainly recognise the organisation UNICEF (United Nations International Children's Emergency Fund). There have been many high-profile UNICEF ambassadors over the years, promoting ways of helping to keep the children of the world safe.

For today, in keeping with the theme of children, we could research further into so-called 'Indigo Children', 'Crystal Children' and 'Rainbow Children'. Some of us may have heard these terms and wondered about them, or noticed a significant difference in the way some children behave even at a very young age.

An example is that of a certain three-year old girl attending nursery school for the first time. When the welcoming staff took her coat off to put it on a hook, instead of this child entering the room to sit down and wait for others to arrive, she immediately turned to greet the arriving children and took their coats from them. This was not something taught to this child at home, yet on attending nursery school for the first time she immediately and naturally acted to be of service to others.

It is believed that Indigo Children were born from the 1970s onwards and that they exhibit psychic abilities such as telepathy, psychic empathy or even clairvoyance. Crystal Children were noted around the year 2000 as especially sensitive children who, in some extreme cases, can suffer from sensory overload. They are loving children who like to hug people, animals and trees, and they often have Indigo Children as parents. Then we come to Rainbow Children, being born in the world today, who usually have a Crystal parent. These children are psychic, intuitive and believed to be natural healers. It is still too early fully to understand our Rainbow Children and what their incarnated role is on Earth; however, if they have the family lineage of Indigo grandparents and Crystal parents then perhaps there is something extra special about them.

There is a belief that all the above children are 'Star Children' who have a special purpose here. It is the Rainbow Children who will help us to heal Mother Earth, leading by example, and if we consider the true story above of the three-year old girl helping other children with their coats this may offer an indication.

Perhaps we may have met some of these children through the years and wondered why they made an impact on us at the time. Researching further about them may provide our answer. If we think we may have one of these children within our own family, then our research could provide insights into how we can support them to fulfil their incarnated role. An illuminating book is A I Kaymen's 'Aura Child', telling the true story of her own upbringing as an Indigo Child (also see the entry for 6th August).

Helpful tip: Researching further about UNICEF and its role in helping the children of the world may lead us to take an active role in some of their activities or to make a donation to this very worthwhile organisation.

22nd November – Greetings Goddesses

Greetings goddesses are inspiring and gentle figures that can greet us and our visitors at the entrance to our home. Greetings goddesses are usually in the *Namaste* pose, sending the message to our visitors that "The spirit in me honours the spirit in you." What a wonderful way to greet our visitors and set the tone for our interactions.

Let us find a greetings goddess today to place near our entrance so that our visitors can be met with honourable respect. It may be possible to place a crystal on this figure and selenite or rose quartz would do well for this, offering peace, love and compassion. If struggling to find a Christmas gift for a friend, perhaps a greetings goddess for them may be the perfect solution, along with a rose quartz crystal as well.

24th November – Temperance in Tarot

The major arcana card of Temperance in the Tarot is linked with the astrological sign of Sagittarius. This card often depicts the goddess Iris of Greek myth who was carer to the gods and also goddess of the rainbow. Goddess Iris reminds us to find balance in life so we can restore and recharge our energies. It is recognised that many give so much to others that their energy reserves become depleted, so there needs to be a balance in our lives to avoid burn-out and life becoming difficult.

Some of us may feel we are not 'a whole human being' if not being of service to others and we continue to keep going. But doing too much can leave us physically and psychologically affected, and it is possible to start feeling worthless as we are not fulfilling what we believe we could. We should acknowledge that there are times when we are just so busy that we have no time for ourselves, and putting the needs of others before our own can be detrimental.

So the Temperance card reminds us at this opportune moment to reflect on the balance of our own lives, whether at home or at work. Large companies often encourage their employees to consider their work-life balance. At this time of the year with Christmas not far away with all the many demands this time can place on us, especially those with young families, this is a good moment to make a commitment to consider how to maintain balance in our lives.

Let us consider whether our life is weighted so much in giving to others that there is little time for ourselves and, if so, explore ways of how an improved balance can be achieved.

26th November – Thanksgiving

The American Thanksgiving Day falls on a Thursday around the end of November. This is one of those days when thinking about all that we have in our lives, and being grateful, has a special focus. Let us light a candle, sit quietly and say a prayer of thanks. We can include our gratitude for working through any challenges faced this year, as this was part of the original thanksgiving for the Pilgrims who faced so many challenges before arriving in the New World, let alone the challenges of creating a safe place in which to live.

We should offer our thanks for the opportunities we have had to grow. Then expand our gratitude to include our family, friends, work colleagues, neighbours and spread this out to our local area, county, country and continent and Mother Earth as a whole. It is good to say the prayers in the present tense, for example being grateful for peace in war zones. Let us be adventurous and meaningful in our prayers of gratitude for ourselves and for others.

28th November – The Greek Goddess Athena

The Greek goddess Athena, daughter of Zeus, was the protector of cities, of civilised life and of agriculture. She is linked with the city of Athens and the Acropolis in that city. The olive tree and the owl, reminding us of wisdom, are associated with her. The Emperor in the Tarot deck is often associated with Zeus who informs us that we are old souls and have incarnated many times, gaining much wisdom. This card reminds us to find our own wisdom, which is our inner holy grail in the heart.

Today, let us think about the wisdom we have gained through our knowledge and experiences. Some can 'hide their light under a bushel' or do not consider they have much wisdom, as their self-esteem and confidence has taken a knock. Let's allow our thoughts to trawl through our memories of the wisdom we have achieved through experiential learning. Even those times when we thought silently to ourselves that we might have made mistakes allow us to realise that we do indeed have wisdom, because those decisions were based on our previous experiences and now we remember this for future instances. Let us be proud and confident of our wisdom, protect it from being undermined by others, and also be happy and willing to continue gaining wisdom throughout our lives, sharing it with others when appropriate.

30ᵗʰ November – St Andrew's Day

As well as being the patron saint of Scotland, St Andrew is also the patron saint of Greece, Romania and of Poland. Andrew was one of the first apostles to spread the gospel after the resurrection of Christ. Before he became a disciple, Andrew was a fisherman, an ordinary man carrying out his trade. In today's society there is much adulation of people deemed to be 'celebrities' and our recognition of people completing a day's work to keep their families in shelter, food, warmth and clothing is seen as somehow less of an achievement.

Yet it is the ordinary people who help to keep our countries operating. The times when we notice this most is when the trains or buses are not running, when the electricity is cut, when the postman is late or when we need medical or nursing help. So instead of only paying attention to the ordinary men and women at work when a difficult situation arises, from today let's pay attention to them every day. We can quietly bless them for driving the bus so we can get to work in the dry while it is pouring with rain outside. Bless them for ensuring the telephone and electricity services are efficient. Be thankful for all the ordinary working people and for the contribution they make in our everyday lives. They are not on display on big screens with gleaming smiles or throwing tantrums, they are the back-room people carrying out their work to keep everything ticking along for us all.

December

This is usually a busy month with many activities for both children and adults alike. It is also a time when we can continue with reflections on our past year during evenings in by the fireside.

This is Oak Moon month and we celebrate Bodhi Day, Yule (the winter solstice), the Festival of Epona and New Year's Eve.

2nd December – Mistletoe

Mistletoe is the plant of December. A parasitic plant using deciduous trees as an anchor for growth, it has become very much a part of the Christmas tradition to stand beneath it and kiss. Mistletoe was deemed a sacred plant throughout Europe in ancient times by the Greeks, Romans, Celts and Druids. It was seen as thriving in the depths of winter, producing white berries while the deciduous tree it grew from appeared dead, thus mistletoe became a symbol of life. It also symbolised fertility with the white berry juice associated with semen. It was believed that when harvested the mistletoe would release its energy of the spirit of vegetation and growth for the land and subsequent crops.

Due to extensive commercial harvesting, mistletoe is being lost from our natural woodland habitats. Therefore, instead of weaving real mistletoe into a wreath to celebrate Yule or Christmas, today we can start to create mistletoe using the papier-mâché technique and enjoy this activity with family and friends. The berries can be made from plain white paper and the leaves from the same but painted green when dry. We can then use floristry wire to bind these together and form bunches ready to weave into our garlands and wreaths, and even a small bunch to hang up for the kissing!

4th December – The Iris

Irises are a favourite flower of many people with their very striking shapes and beautiful colours. There is a winter flowering iris, seen from November to February, called iris stylosa which is a lovely shade of blue with yellow near its centre. The indigo-coloured varieties also provide a wonderful display in a vase. At this time, approaching the birth of Christ whom many view as the Light, and the time of Yule when the light of the sun starts slowly to increase its presence in our lives, the colours of our iris flowers can help us think and communicate with a divine lightness.

The blue (throat chakra), indigo (brow chakra) and violet (crown chakra) colours help to encourage our thoughts and communications to have a certain purity to them, to embody the gift of light no matter where we are and no matter with whom we are communicating. Today, let us allow these iris colours to serve our throat, brow and crown chakras by imbuing them with a compassionate consciousness towards Mother Earth and all living upon her.

We could prepare for a short meditation, ensuring that we are well grounded due to working with these three energy centres, and then spend a short while visualising these colours surrounding us and seeping into every part of our bodies, our internal organs and our energy fields. We can imagine them as swirls of colour, gently mixing and circling, perhaps also as swathes and splashes of colour as well as glittering showers forever moving and dancing around us. Stay with this meditation of colours for around five minutes or longer.

Helpful tip: While working with the throat, brow and crown chakras, a haematite crystal placed under our feet will help with grounding.

6th December – Gifts of Kindness

Occasionally, some of us find ourselves a little short of cash and at Christmastime this can be more of a problem because we want to do our best when giving gifts to our families and friends. There is another option to consider today, which reminds us of the well-known hymn 'In the Bleak Midwinter' which has the words, "What can I give him, poor as I am. If I were a shepherd, I would bring a lamb. If I were a wise man, I would do my part. Yet what I can, I give him, give my heart, give my heart."

A gift of 'kindness from the heart' could be, for example, offering to carry out chores for others such as washing the car, babysitting, vacuuming, gardening, shopping, walking the dog, ironing or collecting the children from school. The list is endless and, as we are giving to our family and friends, we will know what they would appreciate most. We can make these gifts of kindness by elegantly writing our offers of help on separate pieces of paper, perhaps decorating the paper and the envelope ready to produce on Christmas Day. The wording for each kindness we give could be along the lines of, "I promise the bearer of this note that I will… Offered in kindness as my Christmas gift to you."

Any number of these can be given to one person and may prove to be really valued by the receiver as they will recognise that you are offering your time, effort and love for them.

8ᵗʰ December – The Hindu Goddess White Tara

Hindus believe White Tara to be very much a radiant and compassionate goddess, helping us to live long and peaceful lives protected from illness. As she is a radiant goddess in these dark winter months, when many people succumb to the winter blues along with coughs, colds and sniffles, let us respectfully make a request of White Tara for her strength and inspiration at this time.

We can support White Tara in this by drinking herbal teas such as echinacea for our immune system, chamomile for calmness and inner peace and by eating foods that will boost our health. When requesting White Tara for her help we could light a gold candle, to reflect her radiance, and then from the candle light an incense stick of frankincense as a cleanser and purifier of our home. In the spring we can light a gold candle again with the specific purpose of thanking White Tara for her support during the winter.

10th December – Thomas Merton

Thomas Merton (1915 – 1968) was a Trappist monk in Kentucky, USA, and many believe he greatly encouraged the exploration of spirituality during the sometimes explosive '60s and '70s. He held the belief that all religions "lead to God, only in different ways, and every man should go according to his conscience." The dogma and doctrine of some religious faiths can make us feel fettered and thus without the ability to experience the wondrous beauty of accessing the path to the Creator, or Source, through other faiths and beliefs. For some this feels extremely limiting as they believe they are able to see the divine in all manner of ways and in many different faiths.

Thomas Merton's phrase above offers us the alternative viewpoint of allowing our conscience to help us understand the options available in our decisions and choices and to decide whether any actions we choose will sit well with our conscience. From today let us think about what Thomas Merton said and use it to help guide our lives, because life must be about living, learning and loving in joy and peace with mankind, the animals and creatures of this wonderful planet.

12th December – Angelology

There are many well-known teachers in this holistic age who say that they see and communicate with angels, such as Diana Cooper, Jackie Newcomb, Jenny Smedley and Lorna Byrne to name a few. However, we shouldn't forget that angels have been seen, heard and sensed throughout the ages and many texts have been created from these contacts. Today, this is the perfect time to take a closer look at angels and their study, known as angelology.

There are many books on the subject of angels, from the artistic perspective, by spiritual teachers guiding us in how to connect, and also books containing many stories of everyday angelic occurrences experienced by the public. We can search the Internet, read books on angels, note how other people recall their angelic interventions, and experiences and enjoy our time in doing so during this perfect month when angels abound.

Helpful tip: A fascinating personal account to start with is Chris Guyon's 'Extraordinary Things Happen to Ordinary People'.

14th December – Feng Shui

The final Feng Shui tip in this book is to find within our home what is broken or not working properly and to mend it! If it cannot be mended, then recycle it in whichever way possible and replace it with another that does work. This includes ornaments, creaking doors, broken blinds, missing buttons, flickering light bulbs, dripping taps and so forth. Broken or improperly working items within the home sends out the energy of 'an uncaring attitude' and this is not desirable at all in Feng Shui. We start a new year shortly and this is an excellent opportunity for these items to be dealt with so that we can literally begin afresh.

16th December – Carolling

This was traditionally a day when Mummers carolled around the villages in days gone by. For today, let's get organised in advance and join some carol singers or perhaps plan a group of family and friends to sing carols in our local area, after which we can donate any monies collected to a worthy cause.

Much has been publicised in recent years about singing, and especially singing in a choir, being uplifting for us. Not only does singing with others bring about a camaraderie of spirit due to the pleasure of being with like-minded people and 'raising our voices to the rafters', the physical knock-on effects are an added encouragement. We may find that our breathing improves and being with others in an enjoyable activity releases feel-good endorphins. We may decide that finding a local choir to sing with is a New Year's resolution to pursue.

18th December – Kinesiology

The word 'kinetic' is from the Latin for movement and so kinesiology is the scientific study of movement. The muscles in our bodies are continuously moving and a kinesiologist is able to monitor the client's muscle movement in response to external triggers and questioning. For example, some people wish to find out whether they are allergic to certain foods or to know which foods are best avoided; a trained kinesiologist is able to elicit this information by muscle testing. In this way all sorts of information – and not just about foods – can be gleaned to aid us in maintaining good physical and mental health.

Try to find a little time to research kinesiology today. It may open up a whole new world in our lives as in time we could, for example, learn to carry out a muscle-test for members of our own family members when introducing them to a new food in order to ensure that the ingredients will not cause any ill-effects.

20th December – Reflection on the Year

Today, let us spend a little time in quiet reflection of this year, considering what we have changed in our lives and whether anything specific helped to influence us in our changes. Sometimes little changes incorporated into our daily life might have snowballed for even greater effect. Our reflections may also lead us to schedule activities for next year that we have been unable to include this year.

We can think about how we felt a few years ago and compare this to our feelings now about ourselves, our lives, our behaviours and also how we feel in general towards others. Sometimes in life, situations can become worse before they improve in order for us to come out the other side a stronger and wiser person, hopefully also at peace with ourselves. Peace and contentment in life is a wonderful position to feel ourselves to be in, for within peace and contentment lie the joy and love we all deserve.

22ⁿᵈ December – A Medieval Carol

The medieval Christmas carol 'The Holly and the Ivy' is a favourite of many people. However, if we pay close attention to the words it is clear that there are several pagan references in its verses. The Holly King is mentioned with the line "The holly bears the crown." Then the winter solstice and the return of sunlight is represented with "The rising of the sun" and Herne the Hunter being accompanied by a deer leads to "The running of the deer."

Today is a good time to think about the ways in which the Christian Church amalgamated ancient pagan beliefs into its own festivals, such as this midwinter festival of Yule. Indeed, many of our Christmas traditions stem from pagan roots such as the Christmas tree; although Prince Albert introduced it to this country when he married Queen Victoria, it was originally a pagan tradition of his native country.

24ᵗʰ December – Christ Consciousness

In the Christian faith, Jesus is believed to be a gift from God to bring 'light' to the world. This light is sometimes known as Christ Consciousness, which for many means: peace in our hearts, joy for all, love of all, healing for our bodies, calmness in our minds, compassion for those who suffer, graciousness in our daily lives, honouring Mother Earth and all living on her, respecting our soul's journey and respecting the journeys of others.

Even if we are not Christian, we could today spend a few moments in stillness and send loving thoughts with the above in mind for those who are sad, ill, poor, lonely, hungry, homeless, terrorised, displaced or imprisoned. We can pray for 'Christ Consciousness' to envelop them and help them in any way possible. When doing so we could light a white candle and say a prayer, perhaps also lighting incense sticks of frankincense and myrrh as these were said to be gifts for the baby Jesus from the Magi.

26th December – The I Ching (or Book of Changes)

This is an ancient Chinese set of oracles, around 4,000 years old, an in-depth form of divination for guiding our everyday lives. It was first attributed to Fu Hsi, one of the 'Three Noble Emperors' and the original interpretations were greatly developed by Confucius and then again in the Sung Dynasty of around a thousand years ago. Even so, and despite the symbolism of its writing, it is remarkably relevant for today's society. Its answers to our questions, whether about spiritual issues or our down-to-earth problems, pose much food for thought and many who encounter the I Ching will then prefer this form of divination to any other. The father of psychoanalysis, Carl Jung, wrote that were he to have his time again he would spend it all studying this ancient system!

The basic structure of the I Ching (pronounced 'Yee Ching') is a set of sixty-four chapters thought to accommodate all human situations: each of these offers a 'hexagram', a six-line diagram consisting of 'broken' (yin) and 'unbroken' (yang) lines. Each chapter gives an overall interpretation of one's situation and then more detailed advice depending on the positions of these lines. This is usually followed by reference to another hexagram, or chapter, which describes the likely outcome of the situation.

There are several methods for creating the individual lines that make up a hexagram, such as throwing three coins and noting the combinations of heads and tails, or even using a pack of cards. Today, we could investigate this divinatory system and seek if it is something that appeals to us and we might like to work with. The reflective practices the I Ching interpretations encourage us in can help us to move forward psychologically, emotionally and spiritually in our lives. This could be something to consider as a new regular practice with the New Year just around the corner.

Helpful tip: The original English translation of the I Ching is that of Richard Wilhelm's work, still considered by many to be the most true to the original despite there being several more recent versions. Some are put off at first by the lyrical and symbolic language of the book. So a good introduction is 'Lighting the Path: how to use and understand the I Ching' by Nigel Peace, an experienced I Ching consultant. This is written in everyday language and gives many real-life examples of questions-and-answers, as well as the first published glossary of the book's esoteric phrases.

28th December – The Devil in Tarot

The major arcana card in the Tarot of The Devil is linked with the astrological sign of Capricorn. This card encourages us to consider whether we are creating our own Hell on Earth! How many of us never attempt new things, our response being "But what if…?" – and then we do nothing at all. We can become our own worst enemy, negatively viewing situations or procrastinating, setting extremely limited boundaries and restricting ourselves unnecessarily. We become stuck in a rut, trapped by our own choosing, dancing to the tunes of others, often waiting for things to go wrong and for self-ful-filling prophecies to reign.

Does any of this ring a bell? If so, then perhaps today we can consider the opposite by changing our negatives to positives, changing our perspectives, loosening and releasing the noose around our neck (that we placed there) and flying free from our cage.

We can achieve this by attempting new activities, being open to thinking that life can be good and positive, accepting new ideas and spreading our wings. Changing our energetic vibration from negative to positive affects all the energy around us and we attract positive vibrations in return.

We are humans living on this planet, sometimes our plans go awry and situations don't always turn out as we wished them to. But this is life. It is helpful for us to accept the sour with the sweet and not treat a difficult situation as justification to bury our heads under the duvet. Today, we can consider if there are certain situations or habitual responses whereby we place the noose around our own neck, and then set about altering this so that we can lead a fulfilling life, continuing to learn and to grow in all manner of ways.

Helpful tip: Perhaps an affirmation can be adopted to help remind us to be more positive such as, "Today I am open to changing my perspective" and use this to reinforce that it is possible to accept alternatives. They may feel daunting at first but being gentle, kind and encouraging with ourselves will help.

30th December – Birch Month
(24th December – 20th January)

At this time of year, we are still in the hibernating frame of mind and although the winter solstice has passed, with the promise of daylight hours increasing, it remains a time for some continued introspection.

Therefore, during this birch month we could contemplate what we can purify and cleanse from our lives. The bark of the silver birch is meaningful as silver represents purity and cleansing. Interestingly, the tradition of 'beating the bounds' (still carried out today by some Councils and landowners) often uses birch branches in the ceremony.

We can light a silver candle and when doing so request guidance. Sit peacefully and contemplate the past year and what we wish to be cleansed of, such as excessive alcohol intake, our reliance on chocolate for comfort, or other habits that we know are bad for us. We can write these on a piece of paper.

As well as thinking about what we wish to be cleansed of, we also think and plan ahead for how we can realistically achieve these objectives in the coming months. It may be that in order to work towards our goals we need to set some boundaries. Birch is associated with boundaries (as above). In setting our boundaries, not only is it necessary to set them for ourselves, we should consider those to be set for others, whilst at the same time being mindful that we do not offend family or friends by doing so. Making changes in our lives become more achievable when we do so with self-compassion and consideration towards others who are also affected by them.

We write on our piece of paper some bullet-points of how to achieve our goals. We then sit for a while and focus on the candle flame, trying to visualise ourselves six months hence when we have cleansed from our way of living those old energies that no longer serve us. Once finished, we burn the paper in the candle flame and snuff out the candle as if waving 'adios' to those old energies.

The Moons and Festivals

January

The name 'Wolf Moon' was probably due to wolves howling during their breeding season in January and February, and interestingly the Sioux tribe called this the 'wolves run together moon'.

The Feast of Carmentalia honours an ancient Roman goddess who was able to look to the past and the future. Hecate was the Greek 'Queen of Witches', sometimes known as the goddess of the crossroads (after whom the crossroads spread in Tarot is named).

February

The 'Snow Moon' is so-called due to many snowfalls this month in the northern hemisphere.

Imbolc is a Celtic celebration of the first signs of spring, when ewes are lambing, and it is also known as Candlemas in the Christian calendar. Aphrodite was the Greek goddess of love, beauty and sexuality (her ancient Roman counterpart being Venus). Maha Shivrati is a Hindu festival to celebrate the deity Shiva. Lupercalia is again Roman, celebrating purification, whilst Terminalia is named after the god Terminus who was associated with boundaries and endings (February being the last month in the Roman calendar).

March

The 'Hawk Moon' is thought to be linked with clarity, the exceptional eyesight of the hawk being relevant.

Eostre and *Shunbun no Hi* are celebrations this month with entries during the March chapter offering explanations for them. Other festivals include Liberalia, when Roman boys reached their manhood, the Feast of Athena for a Greek warrior goddess and the Feast of Rhiannon, a goddess of horses. We also celebrate Mothering Sunday this month in the UK; however, this may well date back to the Middle Ages when Christians attended the 'Mother Church' in their area.

April

The 'Seed Moon' is so named simply because this is the time for planting seeds. There are three ancient Roman festivals this month. Floralia celebrates Flora, goddess of flowers and fertility of the land; Veneralia is for Venus Verticordia who was petitioned for help regarding affairs of the heart; Ceres was goddess of the grain. We also have the Feast of Cybele, the Greek mother of the gods, and the Feast of Walburg celebrating the German Saint Walpurgis who helped to ward off witchcraft. The Norse Nine Nights commemorates Odin hanging from the Tree of Life for nine nights to learn the secrets of the runes.

May

The 'Flower Moon' reflects the proliferation of flowers visible across the land now, and indeed 'Flora Days' are held in several areas to celebrate the fertility of the countryside and the early signs of summer's arrival.

Beltane is a pagan fire festival honouring the Celtic god Bel and the return of summer. Mercuralia is an ancient Roman celebration of Mercury, the god of merchants. The Feast of Pan recognises the Greek god of the wild and of fertility.

June

We have a 'Strawberry Moon' to reflect the ripeness of wild strawberries ready to eat.

The summer solstice is also known as Litha. Vestalia is another ancient Roman celebration, honouring Vesta, the goddess of the hearth. The Feast of Hera is for the Greek queen of the gods whilst Sigurdsblot celebrates a dragon-slayer of Germanic origin.

July

The 'Hay Moon' is a common name for this month's full moon because in olden days this was the time for harvesting hay. However, with more modern farming methods country folk consider June hay to be the best for horses and livestock.

We have the Feast of Ceridwen, a Welsh deity possessing the cauldron of inspiration, Neptunalia for the Roman god of the waters (whose Greek counterpart was Poseidon) and the Feast of Sulis, celebrating a Romano-British goddess of springs.

August

This month we have the beginning of the wheat harvest, hence a 'Barley Moon'.

In honour of the harvest, we celebrate Lammas, derived from the Anglo-Saxon *loafmass* and also known as Lughnasah after the Gaelic god Lugh. Another link with Lammas and the wheat harvest is Frey Faxi, after Freyr. Raksha Bandham is a Hindu celebration of the bond between brothers and sisters, also associated with protection. The Festival of Torches, Nemoralia, was held in ancient Roman times for Diana, goddess of the hunt.

September

The 'Harvest Moon' is self-explanatory. Crops are often gathered very late into the night, thus some country folk still call this moon 'the parish lantern'.

Mabon is the pagan name for the autumn equinox. Ludi Romani was a Roman games festival, often involving races to portray victories in war, whilst the Festival of Fides honoured the goddess of trust and faith.

October

Our ancestors would now prepare meat from the hunt for the coming winter, so we have the 'Hunters' Moon'.

We celebrate Samhain (or Hallowe'en) this month, the last harvest when nuts are gathered, also honouring our ancestors and the thinning of the veil between the living and the dead. Gandhi Jayanti is held in recognition of the great Mahatma Gandhi. The Roman Meditrinalia was a festival celebrating the new wine vintage, offered as a gift to the gods.

November

There is a 'Frost Moon' this month as night-time temperatures dip.

There are lots of festivals to warm us up, starting with All Saints' Day closely followed by All Souls' Day, honouring the Christian saints and then all the souls in Heaven. Martinmas is for St Martin, originally a Roman soldier, and the Feast of St Cecilia recognises the patroness of musicians. We have Dia de las Muertos (the Day of the Dead), a Mexican celebration for family and friends who have died, and the Feast of Wodin, the god Odin in Norse mythology and god of the dead. The Makahiki Festival is an ancient Hawaiian New

Year celebration, linked with the god Lomo. Finally, the Festival of the Luantishees is for the fairies who are said to guard the blackthorn tree.

December

The 'Cold Moon' speaks for itself, as winter begins in the northern hemisphere.

As well as Yule, the winter solstice when sunlight begins to lengthen our days, there is the Mass of Christ (Christmas) in the Christian calendar. Bodhi Day is when Buddhists celebrate Siddhartha Gautama gaining enlightenment beneath a Bodhi tree. The Festival of Epona recognises a Gallo-Roman protector of horses.

And then of course we have New Year's Eve (Hogmanay in Scotland) when we celebrate the start of a new year and do it all over again...

Bibliography

Ralph Blum	The Book of Runes
James Bowen	A Street Cat Named Bob
Sylvia Browne	Past Lives, Future Healing
Ruth Burgess	A Book of Blessings: and how to write your own
Tiffany Crosara	The Fool's Journey (guided CD)
Liz Dean	Switchwords: how to use one word to get what you want
Robert Dinwiddie	A Little Course in Astronomy
Jo Dunbar	The Spirit of the Hedgerow
Gill Edwards	Living Magically: a new vision of reality
Diana Gabaldon	Outlander
Chris Guyon	Extraordinary Things Happen to Ordinary People
Judy Hall	Earth Blessings; also, The Ultimate Guide to Crystal Grids
Louise Hay	You Can Heal Your Life
Anne Jirsch	Instant Intuition
A I Kaymen	Aura Child
Kwok Man-Ho	Chinese Horoscope Library
Daphne du Maurier	The House on the Strand
Claire Nahmad	Make Your Own Blessing Scrolls
Neal's Yard	Healing Foods: eat your way to a healthier life
Dr Michael Newton	The Journey of Souls

Clinton Ober et al	Earthing
Joseph Ostrom	Auras: what they are and how to read them
Nigel Peace	Lighting the Path: how to use and understand the I Ching
Pierre Pradervand	The Gentle Art of Blessing; also, 365 Blessings to Heal Myself and the World
J K Rowling	Harry Potter and the Philosopher's Stone
Sarah Truman	Haunted by Past Lives
Derek Walters	The Chinese Astrology Bible
Ann Worwood	The Fragrant Pharmacy; also, The Fragrant Heavens

If you have enjoyed this book...

Local Legend is committed to publishing the very best spiritual writing, both fiction and non-fiction. You might also enjoy:

THE HOUSE OF BEING
Peter Walker (978-1-907203-26-4)

A powerful collection of acutely observed verse by a master of his craft. He shows us the mind, the body and the soul of what it is to be human in this glorious natural world, looking deeply beneath the surface of life and writing with sensitivity, compassion and often with searing wit and self-deprecation.

It is a collection that the reader will want to return to again and again, seeing something afresh each time in the formation of a phrase, in a certain pause and in the choice of an exact word. Every one of us will learn something new here about the nature of being.

Winner of the 2018 Local Legend national Spiritual Writing Competition.

A UNIVERSAL GUIDE TO HAPPINESS
Joanne Gregory (ISBN 978-1-910027-06-6)

Joanne is an internationally acclaimed clairaudient medium with a celebrity contact list. Growing up, she ignored her evident psychic abilities, fearful of standing out from others, and even later, despite witnessing miracles daily, her life was difficult. But then she began to learn the difference between the psychic and the spiritual, and her life turned round.

This is her spiritual reference handbook – a guide to living happily and successfully in harmony with the energy that created our universe. It is the knowledge and wisdom distilled from a lifetime's experience of working with spirit.

THE QUIRKY MEDIUM

Alison Wynne-Ryder (ISBN 978-1-907203-47-3)

Alison is the co-host of the TV show *Rescue Mediums*, in which she puts herself in real danger to free homes of lost and often malicious spirits. Yet she is a most reluctant medium, afraid of ghosts! This is her amazing and often very funny autobiography, taking us 'backstage' of the television production as well as describing how she came to discover the psychic gifts that have brought her an international following.

Winner of the Silver Medal in the national Wishing Shelf Book Awards.

SIMPLY SPIRITUAL

Jacqui Rogers (ISBN 978-1-907203-75-6)

The 'spookies' started contacting Jacqui when she was a child and never gave up until, at last, she developed her psychic talents and became the successful international medium she is now. This is a powerful and moving account of her difficult life and her triumph over adversity, with many great stories of her spiritual readings. The book was a finalist in The People's Book Prize national awards.

AURA CHILD

A I Kaymen (ISBN 978-1-907203-71-8)

One of the most astonishing books ever written, telling the true story of a genuine Indigo child. Genevieve grew up in a normal London family but from an early age realised that she had very special spiritual and psychic gifts. She saw the energy fields around living things, read people's thoughts and even found herself slipping through time, able to converse with the spirits of those who had lived in her neighbourhood. This is an uplifting and inspiring book for what it tells us about the nature of our minds.

A SINGLE PETAL

Oliver Eade (ISBN 978-1-907203-42-8)

Winner of the first Local Legend national Spiritual Writing Competition, this page-turner is a story of murder, politics and passion set in ancient China. Yet its themes of loyalty, commitment and deep personal love are every bit as relevant for us today as they were in past times. The author is an expert on Chinese culture and history, and his debut adult novel deserves to become a classic.

5P1R1T R3V3L4T10N5

Nigel Peace (ISBN 978-1-907203-14-5)

With descriptions of more than a hundred proven prophetic dreams and many more everyday synchronicities, the author shows us that, without doubt, we can know the future and that everyone can receive genuine spiritual guidance for our lives' challenges. World-renowned biologist Dr Rupert Sheldrake has endorsed this book as "…vivid and fascinating… pioneering research…" and it was national runner-up in The People's Book Prize awards.

TAP ONCE FOR YES

Jacquie Parton (ISBN 978-1-907203-62-6)

This extraordinary book offers powerful evidence of human survival after death. When Jacquie's son Andrew suddenly committed suicide, she was devastated. But she was determined to find out whether his spirit lived on, and began to receive incredible yet undeniable messages from him… Several others also then described deliberate attempts at spirit contact. This is a story of astonishing love and courage, as Jacquie fought her own grief and others' doubts in order to prove to the world that her son still lives.

Further details and extracts of these and many
other beautiful books may be seen at

www.local-legend.co.uk

www.ingramcontent.com/pod-product-compliance
Lightning Source LLC
Chambersburg PA
CBHW071215090426
42736CB00014B/2839